BEHAVING
AS IF THE GOD IN ALL LIFE
MATTERED

BEHAVING
AS IF THE GOD IN ALL LIFE
MATTERED

UPDATED AND REVISED

Machaelle Small Wright

PERELANDRA

CENTER FOR NATURE RESEARCH
JEFFERSONTON, VIRGINIA
1997

THIRD EDITION

Copyright © 1983, 1987, 1997 by Machaelle Small Wright

Excerpts from *To Hear the Angels Sing,* by Dorothy Maclean
(Lorian Press, 1980), used with permission.

Photographs by Clarence Wright.

Manufactured in the United States of America
Designed by James F. Brisson
Cover design by James F. Brisson
Edited by Elizabeth McHale
Desktop publishing layout by Amy Shelton

Published by Perelandra, Ltd.
P.O. Box 3603
Warrenton, VA   20188

Printed on recycled paper.

Library of Congress Catalog Card Number: 96-072489
Wright, Machaelle Small.
Behaving as if the God in All Life Mattered

ISBN: 0-927978-24-5

6 8 9 7

To David

CONTENTS

PREFACE

It has been quite an eyeopening experience for me to read something I wrote sixteen years ago and to compare it with what I know about the subject today. When I first wrote *Behaving as if the God in All Life Mattered* in 1981, I poured my heart and soul into the project. When I finished writing, I couldn't imagine anything else I would have to say about the things in this book. Well, I am pleased to report that we really do continue to learn and grow. What a difference sixteen years can make! This revised and updated edition of *Behaving* is a celebration of our continuing education and growth.

Of course the facts about my early life in Part 1, "Entering the Monastery of the Streets" have not changed. I must admit that for a fleeting moment I considered inventing a whole new life with a completely different cast of characters just for the sheer joy of it. And it would be kind of fun to see the reactions of the readers who have previously read *Behaving*. But I controlled my cheekiness and kept the story straight. However, I added a few pieces of information and made some word changes that I feel make the story clearer. And I included an update at the end of Part 1 in response to the requests of readers who wrote asking how my life with my parents was ever resolved.

As with my personal history in Part 1, the facts of my first-year co-creative garden in Part 2 ("What's This Crap about Fairies?") also did not change. In writing about this very special time in my life, I use the words I wrote in the original *Behaving* so that the simplicity and even innocence of that summer is maintained. Looking back, I can clearly see that I was a young woman just starting a co-creative relationship with nature, and that this first-year garden was a very special beginner's classroom. Any wording that I changed for this edition was a result of the deeper perspective and understanding I have gotten over the past sixteen years that has allowed me to "say it" more clearly.

Part 3 ("The Lessons Continue") is where that sixteen-year difference surfaced in full and shined. In this section, I have included what I wrote for *Behaving* in 1981, and then I have added new material about what I understand about that particular subject now. I was especially pleased to find that nothing I understand now contradicts what I perceived and understood then, even though my present perceptions and understanding, for the most part, have expanded well beyond what I originally wrote. In actuality, when I reread Part 3 of the earlier *Behaving*, I knew for certain it was time for an updated edition—and I felt that everyone was ready for more information, whether they have read *Behaving* before or not. We've *all* changed over the past sixteen years.

In the last sections, I have improved and clarified the different exercises (Part 4) and updated the "Perelandra Today" information (Afterword). Since the original publication of *Behaving*,

Perelandra has expanded in its size and in the scope of work going on here.

As you can see, I was often struck by the sixteen-year period as I revised *Behaving*. The writing of the original edition of the book began the period and this edition ends it. The time between connects the starting and end points and contains all the life experiences that led me from the first point to the present one. The fact is, we've all moved through a sixteen-year period. If you want to take a moment to appreciate how much experience and change is packed into life, think back to what you were doing and thinking in 1981 and compare that with where you are now. It's quite a trip. May the next sixteen-year period be just as eventful and full of life for you as this past period has been for me. I guess if I'm still around in the year 2013, I'll have to revise and update *Behaving* again. Maybe then I'll rewrite the story of my early years.

Machaelle Wright
Perelandra
1997

INTRODUCTION

Behaving as if the God in All Life Mattered is a book about the intelligent world of nature we traditionally know as devas and nature spirits and about the need for us to change our relationship with that world and, ultimately, our relationship with the planet. I emphasize the word *need*, for without the understanding of the need, we'll never have the energy and drive to make the changes in consciousness and action I am suggesting in this book.

We live in a world of high technology and expertise. We have countless teams of exceptionally qualified research scientists who are dedicated to finding the answers we need in order to live a healthier life on a healed and thriving planet. We look to these people to tell us what we can do in our lives in order to achieve that healthier life on a healed planet. Yet I am saying that, despite all this earnest technology and research, what we need to do now is turn our attention to nature itself, recognize the intelligence inherent in all natural form on Earth and allow it to teach us what we need to know in order that we may apply that information to our lives and our technology, and pull ourselves out of the present ecological mess.

The nature intelligence I speak of contains within it truth—a truth that has been present and available to us since the beginning of time. It is not available exclusively to the gifted. It is a vast universal truth that is present around us everywhere. Our doorway to this truth is through nature itself. Many have opened the doors. Individuals such as myself who live in tiny rural areas around the world, such as Jeffersonton, Virginia, have tapped into the truth within nature purely because of a personal need to understand something more about life. On a larger scale, we have the Findhorn Community in Scotland, which began its growth and development in the 1960s on a foundation of discovery of the co-creation between man and nature. But these examples only serve as affirmations to you that, indeed, there is truth, and it is available to us all, no matter who we are and where we live.

I first consciously tapped into this truth in 1976 when, after a series of events which I share with you in this book, I decided I wanted to become a student of nature and be taught by nature. I immediately discovered that there is an extraordinary intelligence inherent in all forms of nature—plant, animal, mineral, etc.; that contained within this intelligence are the answers to any question we could possibly have about nature—its specific rhythms, its true ecological balance, how this balance can be achieved with the help of humans (and in some cases, despite our interference), the deeper role nature plays on Earth, its various relationships with mankind. This information is just sitting there for us. All we have to do is decide we want to hear it—which can at times be a gutsy decision on our part, since what nature has to teach is not always the easiest thing for us to take in—and to learn how to tap into and receive the information.

I also quickly learned that the desire of the intelligences within nature to connect with us, to communicate and work with us, is intense. The quality of our life and of all life forms on Earth depends on our willingness to learn how to act and move in such a way that we enhance life quality, not damage or destroy it.

In a recent session with the Overlighting Deva of Perelandra, I passed along a question that had been asked of me: "If I were to ask you 'Why is it seemingly so important for humanity to re-connect spiritually to planet Earth now,' what would you say?"

OVERLIGHTING DEVA OF PERELANDRA

I would emphasize to you the word "survival" in answering a question such as this one. But I would be quick to point out that I don't mean survival in the traditional sense you humans tend to understand. You see survival as the opposite of death. We don't recognize death as a reality, therefore we don't use survival in the same context.

By survival, we mean the act of maintaining the fusion and balance between spirit and matter on the physical planet Earth. There is no death, in that spirit does not suddenly cease to exist. Spirit is timeless and shall exist for all eternity. But on Earth, the primary thrust is to fuse in balance spirit and matter. There-fore, to separate spirit from that form is to go contrary to the very purpose of the planet within the larger universal community.

If mankind, through either ignorance or arrogance, succeeds in separating all spirit from form on Earth, he will not render

the planet out of existence. He will only shift its level of exist-
ence. This change will not take Earth's purpose from it. It will
not suddenly be excused, shall we say, from ultimately demon-
strating to all universal levels of reality the celebration of unlim-
ited spirit seated into and reflecting from perfect five-senses
form. If such a disastrous shift should occur, mankind will only
have succeeded in making a challenging job that much more
challenging.

We were always meant to work in partnership—we of nature
and man. The very physical existence of man on Earth has de-
pended upon all kingdoms of nature. In short, the very fact that
man and nature co-exist on the planet has partnership inherent
in it. The partnership, prior to these present changing times, has
developed and grown. Quite often, man has been reluctant to ac-
knowledge this fact. The force behind our partnership has al-
ways been the discovery of what must occur between man and
nature for spirit and matter to be fully fused in balance. From
the moment man and nature came together on the planet, this
link between us has not changed.

Times, however, have changed. The partnership, as with every-
thing else, must be modernized and brought into the present
time. It must shift from being one of distant benevolence, as it
has been in the best of past times, to being one of conscious co-
creativity. This must happen in order to move forward in the
demonstration of that which is Earth's purpose, break down the
barriers that you have built between us and work with us in a
new partnership.

Humans do not, on the whole, understand the dynamic rela-
tionship between spirit and matter. Nature does. It is a dynamic
that is inherent within the life force of nature. But in order for

*the dynamic to be fully useful to all other levels of reality within
this universe, it must be unlocked from its custodianship within
nature and linked with the human tool of intelligence. Only then
can it be applied in principle within all realms of life. That
which is nature is powerful beyond your imagination. And that
which is human is also powerful beyond your imagination. Man
and nature, come together as we have on this planet, hold the
promise and potential of many times their individual power, if
only they can work together to unlock that which nature holds
and infuse the human ability to create expanded usefulness
through the tool of applied intellectual knowledge.*

*If humans continue their reluctance to join us in the partner-
ship we are suggesting, then surely out of human ignorance and
arrogance, we will all continue to experience difficult challenges
to our survival and, eventually, we will be faced with the full
separation of spirit from matter on this planet.*

Along with sharing my work with nature and the results of
that work, I have included a section on my personal history. I do
this so that you can see that there was a logical progression in
my life that brought me to the point where I could accept the
reality of nature intelligences.

And that brings me to the more important reason I have included my history. We *all* have a logical progression. I call it the
spiritual thread that runs through life. Our personal history is a
series of events, some of them subtle, some traumatic. We tend to
look at these events in an emotional light. What hurt me? Who
hurt me? Who took away my chances? etc., etc. I feel this is a
natural and necessary process when dealing with our past. Certainly, I've experienced emotional pain in my own life. But I

don't think this is the only way to look at what's happened to us. In this book, I took a series of significant events in my life (by no means is this a complete record of my history, since a detailed autobiography was not my goal) and looked at each event from a different angle. I looked for that spiritual thread. Instead of asking why something had to hurt and take so much away from me, I asked what this thing, this event, this person gave to me that was necessary in order for me to get to my present position. It was as if I was looking through a kaleidoscope, with each event being one of the colored pieces. I turned the kaleidoscope slightly and the same pieces, the same events, shifted, forming a new pattern. That's where I found the spiritual thread. It was connecting this new pattern.

If a person believes me to be different, to be special, part of an elite mystical group, then he will believe himself to be incapable of exploring and understanding what I have to pass along about nature. He has created a separation between us and declared himself a lesser human than I. Well, horse hockey. We all have the spiritual thread. We all have that logical progression, whether it be traumatic or gentle, that moves us from point A through points B, C and D, all the way to one point where, suddenly, we are faced with a world we didn't know existed. None of us arrives at that point by accident.

I offer this search for the spiritual thread in my life as an example for you to use when looking back into your own life. I can't adequately express how wholeheartedly I recommend this exercise for anyone. For me, it went a long way to ease, at times even eliminate, the state of duality in my life—looking at something as being right or wrong, good or bad, necessary or unnecessary. By seeking the spiritual thread, I saw the purpose contained within the individual events and how each event was built on top of the previous ones, creating a pattern of oneness, wholeness. I saw the light of synthesis. The result has been that more and more I don't look back in anger and disappointment—instead, I look back in gratitude, even celebration.

BEHAVING
AS IF THE GOD IN ALL LIFE
MATTERED

1

Entering the Monastery of the Streets

It STARTED OUT normal enough. Only child, born in 1945 to a young couple living in Baltimore, Maryland. Mother beautiful. Father dedicated to making a success out of himself. Both bought into the "Dick and Jane Concept of Reality," which was passed on to the daughter.

I remember feeling safe and secure with my parents Dorothy and Isadore, our maid, our German Shepherd dog Mark (known for eating anyone who dared to look at me the wrong way), my two pet white mice and all my friends in the neighborhood. I became an accomplished roller skater, except for one minor detail: I couldn't stop without sitting down on the asphalt. I went to the movies with the gang every Saturday. In kindergarten, I eloped with my true love—to his house. I was returned by his parents and spanked by mine.

It was also at this time that I began to develop my unusual relationship with the Catholic Church. I was born into a Jewish family. What did *I* know about the inner workings of the Catholic Church? Every morning as I walked to school, I knocked one block off my trek by cutting diagonally through a Catholic church. On the way, I passed a huge bank of lighted votive candles. For some reason, I decided that it was dangerous to leave the candles burning, so every morning for one year, I blew them out.

I moved through first grade without incident. Toward the end of the school year, my parents announced that we were selling our house and moving to the country. Isadore was quickly moving up the ladder of success and had discovered a new passion—horses. We were now to have a house befitting our status and enough land for my father to pursue his passion.

Early that summer, we packed up ourselves, the maid and the dog. The white mice and a bunch of their babies escaped from their cage and took up residence in the basement. We never found any of them, and my parents moved from our row house with great glee over having left a basement full of white mice for the new owners. And so we moved to the country.

It was here that the "Dick and Jane Concept of Reality" began to crumble.

Dorothy had enjoyed her life and friends in the city. I learned much later that she was a shy woman, which she covered with a veneer of snobbishness, and a disturbed woman—neither of which surfaced until after we moved. Unfortunately for me, one of the things she was disturbed about was having a child. She didn't enjoy children and did not appreciate being left alone with one. I no longer had the usual inner-city neighborhood to occupy

4

my time outside the house, so I spent much of my time during the first months in the country sitting around trying to figure out what someone living in the country did for entertainment. My presence made Dorothy tense. Our maid, bless her, saw what was happening and took over much of my care and feeding, anything that gave my mother a little space from me.

To add to Dorothy's loneliness, Isadore, who was now a successful traveling salesman in the garment industry, was spending three months at a time on the road. He would return for three weeks, devote most of his time to his horses, argue with Dorothy about her habit of writing checks without filling out the stubs and then leave again for another three months.

It was during this time that the three of us unconsciously isolated ourselves from one another. Dorothy cut herself off from me, except to perform the barest of parental duties, and tried to find something to occupy her time until Isadore came home from his trips. She wasn't very creative about it. She watched soap operas on TV. In the winter she sewed. But she had a rule that if she couldn't finish what she was working on in one day, she would never pick it up again. She had a lot of unfinished clothes lying around. In the summer, she bought plants from a local greenhouse, set up a flower bed and spent hours every day weeding. It wasn't that she enjoyed working with flowers so much as it was her determination to have a good tan. She decided that if she stayed out in the sun long enough, her freckles (of which she had many) would run together and form one big tan that would never fade.

Isadore would return home from his trips, change his clothes and go to the stable to work with his horses. His passion for horses equaled his passion for making money. He was going to train himself to be the best rider with the best trained hunters and open jumpers in the country. In the beginning, Dorothy rode with him, but she didn't share his passion. One day after an argument, she stopped riding altogether.

Our maid buffered me from most of the tension and isolation that developed between my parents. But she still had other duties around the house, and I had a lot of time to be alone.

I began to develop an interior life by letting a secret world grow inside me—a world that gave me pleasure and excitement. My room became my womb. The eight acres of woods behind our house became my secret safe place, my friend. I would play games where I would see myself as an Indian traveling through the woods on foot for thousands of miles, going to my new homeland. (In 1988, I discovered that Dorothy was half Native American—a fact she had never talked about. Her mother, who died during my mother's birth, was Hopi.) I was always running from the white soldiers who were never far behind, so it was important to move through the woods without making a sound. I spent hours tiptoeing and moving my body through tight spots without disturbing one leaf. Then I'd climb trees to see if the soldiers were on my trail. I became quite adept at entertaining myself. It was something I shared with no one—certainly not my parents.

As soon as I learned to write, I began recording my adventures. I also began to write about my fantasies—strange places and people I would experience when I sat quietly by myself. I recorded the sounds and the smells, the strangeness of the environment. I didn't know where these places were. There was nothing about them that was familiar to me. I just assumed they were fantasies and that everyone had them. It wasn't until I was twenty-eight years old that I found out that these childhood fantasies were actually astral travels.

During the summer between second and third grades, Isadore decided it was time for me to learn how to ride a horse. Dorothy had stopped riding and he needed another "body" to help exercise the horses. So he gave me Dorothy's horse—a big, gentle 16-1/2 hand, half-breed hunter named Freedom.

I had been afraid of this horse for a year because he was so big and played with our new dog by grabbing the back of her neck with his teeth and slinging her onto his back. The dog would scramble to her feet, and he'd carry her around the field like a circus pony. I was afraid that he would grab *me* by the neck if I walked too close to him. In second grade, our school counselor gave the class one of those ghastly personality formation tests in which one question was: "What are you most afraid of?" I, of course, answered "Freedom." Well, my teacher, the counselor and the principal became somewhat alarmed and called my parents to school for an emergency meeting about this strange child who was afraid of "freedom." McCarthyism was running rampant at the time, and I think my parents thought the school authorities figured we were communists! Isadore cleared. up the misunderstanding quickly—and about six months later he gave me the horse as a gift. I'm not sure if it was a reward or a punishment.

The first thing I decided about Freedom was that I did not want to fall off him—I thought the sheer distance would kill me. For the next three or four years, this was the guiding motivation that kept me glued to that horse.

There is an old adage about it being disastrous for wives and children to be taught by their husbands and fathers. Being taught to ride by my father fit this adage.

He started me on a program that had as much drive, dedication and discipline as the one he had developed for himself. He was demanding and impatient, and, somehow, due to my nervousness, I was able to prove to him time and time again that his daughter was an imbecile. He would yell out a command, I would choke, do the exact opposite, and he'd threaten to take the horse away if I didn't pay attention. Each day, for two or three hours, he'd plunk me on this animal and we'd go through the same tense routine. (What neither one of us knew at the time was that I suffered from dyslexia. Isadore would shout for me to turn the horse's head to the left, my brain would go blank and I'd invariably turn Freedom's head to the right. Dyslexia.)

One day I noticed that when Isadore shouted a command, the horse would automatically start to do whatever was shouted. Freedom had been trained to follow voice commands and I hadn't known it! If I just sat on the horse and let him react to whatever Isadore was shouting, I wouldn't make any more mistakes.

Brilliant move. And it worked. The tension between my father and me decreased dramatically. I doubt that he thought I had made a miraculous breakthrough, or that I had suddenly become clever and smart. All along he had been telling me that the horse was smarter than I was. But I think from this point on, he appreciated the fact that I was beginning to understand just how much smarter this horse was.

I spent nearly every day riding for seven years. In the beginning, I rode Freedom while I learned the fundamentals. As I became more accomplished, Isadore put me on other horses. I spent hours riding in a ring—riding in a circle. My friends at school also had horses, and they talked about going out together on long rides through the woods around the countryside. My father wouldn't let me do that. It was too dangerous. Horses were serious business. I could fall off doing something stupid; I could kill myself. As if to accentuate the issue, one of my girlfriends hopped on her Shetland pony while it was grazing in the field. Something spooked the pony, causing it to wheel around and bolt. She fell off—she wasn't wearing a riding helmet—her head hit a rock and she lay in a hospital, deteriorating into a vegetable.

So I continued riding in circles.

Due to a lack of more frivolous options, my focus turned to the notion of excellence: I wanted to do everything with the horse as perfectly as possible. It became intriguing—a constant puzzle, a game. What were the horse and/or I doing wrong that made a movement slightly off? When we did hit perfection, I could tell the difference in the quality of movement. And eventually, riding in a circle became fun.

I came away from this intense experience with my father with a number of useful things: One, a sense of accomplishment—I became an excellent rider. I overcame my fear of Freedom. And I had not fallen off! I also experienced what it meant to strive for excellence—and to achieve it. Now I knew what it was to focus my energies in a disciplined manner. And I learned how to get inner joy and satisfaction out of something that looked tedious.

I learned all of this by the time I was twelve.

A few years after I started riding, our maid had to leave. She had been living in our home during the weekdays and returning to her family for the weekends. Someone got sick—her husband or son—and she was needed in her own home. I was very sad to see her go. But even though I considered her a friend and a surrogate mother, I was more frightened about what would happen if she wasn't there to buffer me from my parents.

For awhile it wasn't bad. Isadore's business trips changed, and now he was away for three weeks at a time instead of three months. He also became very involved with the horse crowd—hunting, parties, horse shows. Although Dorothy didn't ride, just going to the shows, giving the parties and being around new people gave her some sense of direction in her life. She seemed not to be as lonely.

But these people were heavy drinkers, and during this period she started drinking—something she hadn't done before. So now during the summer, instead of weeding and trying to make one big freckle of her body, she would lie in the sun and drink mint juleps while going for her big freckle.

We all went into a new level of isolation from one another. Dorothy fell more and more deeply into the bottle. Isadore created personal goals with his horses that caused him to become even more single-minded in that area of his life. At the same time, he made a business shift. He decided to buy out the company he had been working for and make the business his. His life was now totally divided between business and horses. It was Dorothy's job, as his wife, to take care of the house (she could hire the maid of her choice) and the children (of which there was only one).

For me to survive in this environment, I had to retreat deeper inside myself. Riding still occupied much of my free time. I concentrated on getting very good grades and took on as many school-related activities as possible. During those hours when I was alone, I had my inner adventures. I developed a new level of quiet and fascination at what "popped into my fantasies," and each night I recorded them in a journal.

Everything went into my journals—my fantasies, observations about the people I had met, my fears, angers, problems, desires. By the time I was twelve, I had developed an outlet for all the things going on inside me—an outlet that gave me a wonderful sense of emotional release because I could "say" anything I wanted without fear of outside judgments. Through this process, I experienced and developed a sense of inner freedom despite external limitations and pain.

A bird in flight within a prison—my flight was inward.

Dorothy became a full-fledged alcoholic by the time I was ten. Alcoholism was not an upper middle class issue in the mid-1950s. It was seen as an affliction that poor people and bums had. So all the warning signs Dorothy sent out were ignored. Isadore had the extraordinary ability to see only what he wanted. (Many years later, I brought up the issue of Dorothy's early years of drinking, and he told me that he hadn't noticed she had been drunk every day for the last two years they were together. I believed him. He had the ability to be that tunnel-visioned.)

Her behavior became increasingly erratic—especially toward me. The alcohol brought to the surface the anger she had about having a child, and she began doing strange things to me— twisted things. If she caught me lying on the living room rug watching TV, she would stand on my hair, so that I couldn't move my head, and slowly spit on my face. Although I was just a child, even I figured out that this behavior was strange. None of my friends talked about their parents doing these things. She also took out her frustrations by trying to bean me on the head with a

11

cast iron skillet, by pushing my face and hands into vats of hot food, forcing me to eat until I threw up, putting me through strange psychological tests that, when I failed, caused her to send me to my room for long periods of time. (That punishment I liked.)

Interspersed with these activities, she would come to me weeping, telling me how much she loved me—which I accepted, since in the "Dick and Jane Concept of Reality," mothers love their children.

On the whole, I responded to her by hiding as much as I could. I increased my school activities even more, spent more hours in journal writing and escaped into my inner adventures. Other than to hide, I didn't know what to do about my mother.

The environment in the house took on a feeling of intense pressure. No one was talking to anyone. We weren't even saying good night to one another. Each of us kept up a facade by keeping very active. My parents continued to have weekly parties. By now, Dorothy was becoming more overt with her strange actions. Of course, she was always drunk, but now she was becoming sloppy about it in public. She'd be sarcastic—even downright nasty—to the people who were invited to the parties. She'd tell someone their prized, darling little child was actually a royal pain in the ass. . . .

Looking back on this period, I sometimes feel that my mother was the only sane one in the family. We had created a world of total absurdity, and she finally chose to act it out in absurd ways. The parties were the stuff from which Dorothy Parker short stories sprang. Respectable facades were put up by everyone. Somehow, in her drunken stupor, Dorothy saw through the whole mess and exploded.

It happened at one of those parties. Someone made the mistake of asking her when dinner was going to be served. She was only three hours late. She responded by flinging her martini glass across the kitchen; it hit someone's child (the one she considered to be the greatest royal pain in the ass). She then ran through the house systematically destroying it as she went along. Isadore didn't catch her before she put the chair through the TV, but he did catch a chair in mid-air just as it was about to hit the glass china cupboard.

I sat on the sofa watching all the ashen expressions and hushed, urgent whispers as everyone scurried out of our house and headed for their cars. My mother ended up sprawled on the floor right at my feet with my father straddling her body, trying to keep her from moving. Blood was coming from his face, dripping onto her, as he cried. Dorothy screamed a lot of sailor-like, violent things about Isadore until she passed out.

At least she had gotten his attention.

I slipped into a semi-state of shock—a state I was to stay in for the next eight years. None of this fit into what I thought "family" should be. It was at this point that I seemed to split into two people. One person had an amazing, joyful, powerful, vibrant life going on inside her. The other person took on the somber task of surviving. By this time, I was so used to dealing with my own problems and my own life that it didn't dawn on me to yell for help. If I just hung low for a while and went about my business, this situation would work itself out, and we would all return to the Dick and Jane bit.

It was during this time that I overheard a lengthy and especially loud argument between my parents. They were yelling about divorce and which one of them should have custody of me.

They weren't fighting about who had the right to keep me or who loved me more. They made it clear that neither one of them wanted to keep me. My mother declared she didn't want me around her. And my father kept shouting that he wouldn't know what to do with me, so she better take me. I sat at the top of the stairs listening—and quietly crying.

My world was quickly disappearing. At least I had my school and my room—they were still stable in my life. My routine was still there.

Within a month, Dorothy managed to destroy these last areas of stability. One day I returned home from school to find that she had gone to the lawyer's office, signed divorce papers and wasn't planning to come back. Mind you, I was still in a semi-state of shock—a state that buffered me from the raw, damaging pain that was flying around. I took the news from Isadore like a trooper, put the information into my little "computer" and tried to figure out what this turn of events was going to mean to my life. As far as I could tell, I would still go to school, but I wasn't sure about my room and meals now. I looked to Isadore for some indication that my basic needs would be taken care of. After all, that was still the father's role.

Isadore went into a tailspin. His concept of family had been based on the wife fulfilling her job description. Now he was left with this child—this twelve-year-old—whom he had barely spoken to and had no idea how to care for.

Several people offered to help by taking me into their homes, at least until the school year was out.

The first family could not deal with my periods of quiet. They thought I was very strange. And the mother and four teenagers truly resented the fact that I made friends with the father—a quiet, gentle, highly intellectual man who enjoyed telling me his stories while the rest of the family was elsewhere in the house living their own lives. Together, we formed an unofficial club for outcasts, thus making my living there unacceptable. It was a surprise to me the day Isadore came for me because no one had told me that I would be leaving. That day, everyone in the house disappeared. I left a note saying thank you and good-bye.

The second home had a husband (a friend of my father), a wife who was a teacher (retired) and a baby. The teacher-wife accepted my periods of quiet, and all went rather well until one weekend while the wife was away the husband got drunk and tried to rape me. Somehow I talked him out of it. When the wife returned, she found me more deeply interior, writing away madly in my journal. She must have suspected something, for she came into my room while I was in school and read about the dirty deed in my journal. When I came home that night, Isadore was waiting for me. There was a big confrontation with the husband in which I had to state the charges I had written about in front of him, his wife and my father. He confessed and I was immediately whisked out of that home.

Nothing was ever said to me personally by Isadore about the incident with his friend. I was left to feel that I had somehow failed again. I hadn't even been sure my father believed my story until a few days later when the husband came to our home to speak to him. I listened to the conversation from upstairs. Apparently, Isadore had contacted a lawyer about taking this guy to court on charges—attempted rape, I guess—but he had been advised by the lawyer to drop the idea since taking it to court would have been traumatic for me. The man was most relieved that my father was not going to press charges—he had just found

15

out that his wife was pregnant again. He apologized to Isadore and left.

For the time being, I was back in my own room.

Isadore was actively involved in getting a new wife so that he could put his family back together again. The candidate was his secretary—a woman eight years older than his own daughter. I was looking forward to any kind of re-creation of family so that I could get back to my old, familiar routine. But the new woman was interested in something else. Money. She knew Isadore was about to purchase the company and was on his way to becoming a very wealthy man. The last thing she needed was an heir from another family laying claim to all that money. So while I was looking to her in anticipation of having an "older sister," she was working on ways to get me kicked out of the house and out of my father's life.

Enter Dorothy. My mother had disappeared for six months. Apparently, she had gone through one of her guilt sessions about being such a rotten parent and, in a case of classic timing, called Isadore to ask if I could come live with her. He had been having all kinds of problems and arguments with potential wife #2 about me and decided if he could just get me out of the house long enough to marry her and get her settled down, then he could eventually pull me back into the home—and we could all live happily ever after.

As soon as school ended, I was told to pack—I was going to live with my mother. I was stunned.

I was also told that I could take anything in the house I wanted. I packed all my clothes, my encyclopedia set, all my journal writings, all of our record albums (about ten in number), the portable stereo my father had given me that Christmas and one framed picture. We had a limited-edition series of charcoal sketches of horse scenes throughout the house. I chose my favorite—the one of three mares and three foals in a field. Two foals were having their meal supplied courtesy of their mothers. The third foal and mother were separated, each eating grass—the foal's forelegs straddled so that he could reach the ground. It wasn't until many years later when I dropped the picture, causing the plate to fall out of the back, that I found out the title was "The Rugged Individualist." Without realizing it, I had chosen the picture that symbolized the new stage of life into which I was moving.

The day I left home, I knew I would never return. A heavy sense enveloped me as I took a long look at the house, the woods, the field, Freedom. . . . I knew I wasn't coming back. I was sad and scared. Everything had been taken away from me. My safe, predictable rhythm. My school—the next year I would have to go to another school since my mother lived so far away. The safety of my room. The security that fathers were supposed to provide. My home.

I was thirteen. I had a sense of foreboding about my future. The day I left, I somehow knew that my future was dependent on me and me alone. I wasn't sure what that meant, but I could sense it nonetheless. Consciously, I knew I wasn't qualified to be in charge of my own life. I came away from my father's house with two skills, thanks to our maid. I could scramble eggs and iron handkerchiefs. What I didn't realize was that my years of surviving in the pressure cooker my parents had created had forced me to develop exactly the skills I needed for the stage I was about to enter. I didn't have the external wherewithal to survive—that could be picked up and learned as I went along—but

17

I had the internal strength, the internal makeup to give myself the motivation from inside to survive.

A neighbor—a friend of what used to be our family—drove me to my mother's. Dorothy was living in a resort town on the eastern shore of Maryland, a town called Ocean City. We had gone there as a family every summer for vacation for as long as I could remember. She always liked it more than Isadore did.

I wasn't told much about Dorothy's new life, only that she had a job and an apartment. When I left home, I had, along with my cardboard box and suitcase, $20 that Isadore gave me for the trip and the address of her apartment.

We arrived in the early afternoon. Dorothy met us sporting frosty-blue lacquered fingernails and a new boyfriend. We spent the next few hours in the apartment, Dorothy catching up on all the old home news, all three adults getting drunk as time wore on. I think my mother had genuinely missed me. Even with her drinking, she was still warm and friendly toward me. She boasted to her boyfriend about her beautiful, wonderful child. I found the scene excruciatingly embarrassing.

In late afternoon, the neighbor-friend headed back home, and Dorothy informed me that she and Whatshisname had a dinner date. I could spend the time unpacking and, if I got hungry, there was food in the refrigerator that she had bought just for me that day. She'd be home early, and I was not to let any strange men into the apartment.

She didn't return for three months.

I sat in the apartment for three days waiting, leaving only to take short walks along the beach. My semi-state of shock was becoming more full-fledged as the days wore on. The more I panicked, the quieter I got. And at that point, I was very, very quiet.

After the second day, I tried to call Isadore from a pay phone down the street. (The apartment had no phone.) But the soon-to-be wife #2 answered and told me I shouldn't bother my father, that I was the cause of all their problems and I was to go away and leave them alone. A couple of those phone calls started to significantly eat into my $20, so I gave up trying to reach him, feeling that it was best to save my money for food.

Whenever I've shared this part of my life with friends, they've found it incomprehensible that I managed to survive beyond this point. I was just thirteen. I could not have been more naïve about the world. I was in unfamiliar surroundings. The $20 I had was, for all intents and purposes, no money. And I was alone—cut off from both my parents. But anyone who has been there knows that when you get to this point, some switch inside you shifts, and all of a sudden a force, a deep sense of survival, starts to motivate you into action. Life becomes basic and uncomplicated.

I discovered that I had a strong fear of starving to death. The thought of slowly wasting away alone in some strange apartment terrified me. So that basic drive for survival took over. I needed food, and to get food I needed money. To get money, I needed a job.

That's where the glitch came. I had heard in school that a kid needed a work permit to get a job before age sixteen. I wasn't sure what a work permit was, but I knew parents had to sign it. Since I didn't have the parents around to sign, I decided I'd have to work around it. Luckily, even though I was only thirteen, I was already 5 feet 9 inches tall. So in a matter of minutes, I went from being born in 1945 to being born in 1942, thus solving the age problem.

The next problem was figuring out what kind of job I could get with my dazzling display of handkerchief-ironing and egg-scrambling skills. I was surrounded by restaurants and coffee shops, so I leaned toward the eggs and decided to aim for a waitress job.

The idea of looking for work terrified me, but not as much as starving to death did. One terror overriding the other was the only thing that pushed me out of the apartment.

You're not going to believe this—it sounds much too convenient—but I got lucky on my first try. It was a small coffee shop in a motel. The one and only waitress had quit, and the manager of the motel needed me for the job as much as I needed the job. I fabricated all the information requested on the job application that could prevent me from being hired, figuring the only thing standing between me and eating were those dumb questions.

But then came the problem of the social security number—something I had not heard about before. That's when the manager got a little edgy. He sat down beside me and asked me where I came from and what I was doing in Ocean City. I gave him a song and dance about my parents just divorcing, my father being poor, my mother not getting any money from him to help support us and that we had come here to start a new life. She already had a job but it didn't pay enough, so I needed to get something as well. We had forgotten all about the social security problem, but I promised faithfully to mail away for a card immediately if only he would let me have the job. . . .

Now I admit it's a pretty weak line, but it worked. His pressure to get a waitress before the lunch rush, coupled with my strong determination to eat, won out. He agreed to let me work while I waited for the card. (Luckily, it arrived in two weeks. It may be the only time the government has moved quickly on anything.)

I took the last of my $20 and went to a shop the manager had suggested, bought a uniform and started work that noon.

As a waitress, I was a disaster. It wasn't at all that I was lazy. I shot around the coffee shop like I was in a sprint race. But I had no idea what I was doing, so all of my movements were totally inefficient. I couldn't get the hang of how to organize myself. The customers got their orders, but it usually took me about eight trips to get it to them. They must have felt I had a heart because I got nice tips from the very beginning. The money rolled in—about $8 that first day! That was enough to get a good meal and still have some left over for the next day. Security.

I'd like to say I became a good waitress, but that would be a lie. The cook was an old man who had been a short-order cook since about two years shy of eternity. He flipped pancakes and eggs by throwing them in the air and catching them in the pan. I accepted him as a genius. He knew from the moment I walked into the shop that this was my first job. So, for the first week, he gave me pointers, anticipated my needs, caught me in mid-flight, spun me around and headed me in the right direction. We got to be a pretty good team, as long as he was willing to do his job and half of mine as well.

During the third week, my legs started aching badly. I assumed it was from working. Nothing to worry about. But the pain persisted, and the manager and cook insisted I see a doctor.

It seemed I had growing pains. I had grown too quickly in one spurt, and there was a temporary problem in my joints that my waitress job was irritating. I would have to quit my job. Get something less strenuous. (I covered myself at the doctor's office when he asked where my parents were with the same weak story I had used at the coffee shop. He said he would send the bill to "our" apartment for my mother. At least this gave me some time to get the money together.)

I returned to the coffee shop in a panic—but very quiet on the outside, of course. The owner wasn't there. While I waited, I talked with the girl who guarded the motel pool. She listened as I told her my plight. It turned out that she had wanted the waitress job because she could make more money.

My mind started clicking. I had taken Red Cross swimming lessons back home and had become an excellent swimmer. I had advanced to the Swimmers level by the time I was nine—way ahead in age of all the others. I repeated the Swimmers classes for two years because I was too young to go into the Lifesaving class. But during my last year, they had allowed me to take the class rather than repeat Swimmers again, as long as I understood that I was too young to get a Lifesaving badge at the end. There was no practical reason why I couldn't take a job as a lifeguard. This was a small pool. I could guard it with no problem.

By the time the owner got back, the girl and I had agreed (if he would let us) to trade jobs. I told him what the doctor had said, gave him a demonstration of my lifesaving skills and agreed to get an okay for this job from the doctor.

I was a much better lifeguard than waitress. I only had to go in twice—both times after children who had slipped through their inner tubes. When parents asked if I would give their children private lessons, I figured, why not? I knew those Red Cross lessons by heart. I'd just give them what I had learned and make some extra money on the side, as well.

Those remaining two months of summer turned out fine. I was making enough money for meals—I was even managing to save a little money. I had a job that involved something I enjoyed. And I was getting a great tan.

I tried to call Isadore a couple of times, but it was impossible getting past the woman who was now wife #2. I wrote him several letters asking for help, but she intercepted them. She sent them back with nasty notes recommending that I leave them alone. Trying to get back home—maybe by bus—didn't seem like an intelligent option. I didn't want to spend the money on a bus ticket for a trip that most likely would turn out to be a waste. I'd end up losing my job and the money.

I found out that Dorothy was working as a hostess at one of the hotel lounges. I went to her a couple of times, mainly to tell her that the landlord was looking for the rent on the apartment. But also, I hoped she'd do something or say something that would let me know that she was going to take care of me. Instead, she'd only tell me to go back to the landlord and tell him that she would be by in a few days with the money and that she'd see me then, too—something that never happened, of course.

It wasn't until two and a half years later, when I started learning something about alcoholism, that I realized that Dorothy had been suffering from periods of blackouts during this time. She probably kept forgetting I was in Ocean City or that she had even rented an apartment for us. She was living with her boyfriend who assumed she was taking care of anything I needed. He didn't ask questions. When she blacked out, she could function "normally" in her routine. She simply had no memory of anything that was going on—and the people around her didn't know anything was wrong.

All the circumstances that surrounded Dorothy and Isadore, causing them to cut loose their child, are complicated at best. It's obvious to me now that it was important for my own growth that I remain on my own. Everything and everyone was "conspiring" to keep me from reconnecting in any way with them. I couldn't get the simplest, most basic communication going. I was being stopped in every direction.

At the time, however, I certainly didn't have the benefit of this wonderful understanding of cosmic timing and evolutionary progression. All I knew was that my parents didn't seem to be coming to the rescue, and summer was coming to an end. That meant my job would soon be over and school would begin. The landlord informed me that by the end of September, my mother and I had to be out of the apartment—and that he was still waiting for her to come by with the rent. Somehow, I had been able to stall him with the promise of Dorothy coming with the rent, thus warding off an eviction.

I found out from co-workers that there was one junior/senior high school seven miles away. To get in, Dorothy would have to register me. Rather than try to deal with her, I got one of my co-workers to drive me to school and help me to register. ("I'm sorry my mother couldn't be here. She couldn't get off work. But she asked a friend of ours to come with me in her place. I'd like very much to go to your school. . . .") I think the woman was stunned that a kid was asking to come to school. At any rate, it caught her off guard and she accepted my story. Together, the three of us got me registered. If I didn't know the answer to a question or if the true answer, particularly about my parents, might cause a problem, I simply made up a more acceptable answer.

I didn't consider this lying. I saw it as survival, as doing what needed to be done. I also (and I don't know where I got this idea) feared that if I tipped off anyone in authority about my true situation, they would throw me into a girls' reform school. I knew I had to keep a low profile, and, no matter what, I couldn't attract the interest of anyone in authority. I needed the authorities to think I was a normal kid with a mother who was always working her heart out trying to keep us going.

It wasn't that difficult to keep this facade up in school. As long as papers and report cards were signed on time and returned to the school with a consistent signature, nobody asked questions. Plus, I was an above-average student. I didn't become a behavior problem. They had no cause to pay attention to me.

At the end of the summer, I found another apartment in a small converted house. The owner didn't want the building to stand vacant for the winter. I paid something toward the first rent from my savings and told the new landlady that my mother would be coming with the rest. She didn't buy the story. So I pulled out all the stops to prove to her that I was quiet, neat, reliable and more than willing to be a watchdog for her building. She agreed to let me stay if I was willing to stay without utilities. At that point, electricity was the least of my worries. I got my own place rent-free—right on the beach, facing the ocean.

The next hurdle was money for food during the winter. The motel next to where I was working was staying open all winter. During the summer, I became friends with the teen-aged daughter of their manager, and she convinced her father that I really needed a job—any job. The day after Labor Day (after the pool closed), I was working next door as a switchboard operator.

Need I mention that I had no experience? It was the kind of old-fashioned switchboard with trunks and lines servicing about two hundred rooms, a lounge, several restaurants and a coffee shop. I spent the first week disconnecting and replugging everyone into the wrong lines. A large bankers' convention had filled the motel, and most of the guests were drunk and never quite sure of what was happening to them on the phone anyway. So, thanks to the general vodka haze hovering over the motel, I didn't get many complaints while I learned my new job.

I was set for the winter. School would begin in two weeks. I had a nice apartment and a fine job.

Entering a new school is the same pain for everyone. Inner tension grips us as we deal with new people, new routines, new teachers . . . a bit like being dropped into a foreign country without a map.

Despite the tension, I looked forward to going to school—any school. I didn't like being totally responsible for my life. It was too awesome a job. My only limitations and expectations were the ones I set for myself. It wasn't just a matter of trying to do the "right thing." I had to first find out what the right thing was for each new situation. I was mentally exhausted most of the time. School gave me structure and direction, and for seven hours a day all I had to do was respond to it. After school, I went straight to my job, did my homework between phone calls, went home around eleven o'clock and to bed.

I made friends, really fine friends—kids my own age who had worked in Ocean City for several summers already, making them mature beyond their years. I confided in them what was happening to me, and they tried to figure out ways to help. A couple of them told their parents about me, and I remember hoping that somebody would invite me into their home to be a part of their family.

But I ran into difficulty. Dorothy was becoming a notorious lady around town. Once the season ended, the population went from a quarter of a million people down to about 150—all owners and staff who stayed throughout the winter. Out of this 150, two groups formed. One was the fun-loving hell-raisers who appreciated and welcomed Dorothy's charm. The other was the family-oriented group. My friends were from the families who were part of the latter group. But they knew about Dorothy and felt that getting involved with one of her problems—me—was bound to be messy.

By this time, Dorothy was letting it be known that I was her daughter. But because I was safe in an apartment, working and going to school, her friends assumed she was caring for me. It didn't even dawn on them that anything different was going on. This was during the late 1950s, early 1960s, when people didn't talk about child abuse and neglect as much as they do now. I was naïve, but so, too, were the adults around me. Then, everyone assumed mothers took care of their children, no matter what. Also, in my case, Dorothy kept the pressure off herself by answering any questions about me as if everything were just fine. It was her way of surviving.

Having others know that I was Dorothy's daughter became a mixed blessing during the year and a half I was in Ocean City. Sometimes, when I needed a job or a place to stay and I happened to be dealing with one of Dorothy's friends, they'd give me a break. Any daughter of Dorothy's was a daughter of theirs. But other times, it would backfire on me. Her male friends would assume "like mother, like daughter," and try their best to "hit on me." I spent a lot of energy convincing them that they'd have to go back to Dorothy. This resulted in my going deeper into my shell in an attempt to become more invisible.

That first winter in Ocean City became a test for survival. Within a month after school started, the town was hit with a damaging storm. My first experience with a northeaster—three days of heavy rains and hurricane-like winds. Many of the hotels and motels were destroyed or heavily damaged.

I worked with a couple of my friends around the clock, helping to rescue stranded people. When I returned to the apartment, I found that the ocean had been through at least once, and my possessions were strewn over the surrounding beach. The record player, which was stored high in a closet, was untouched. I lost my encyclopedias and the majority of my clothes but found the records and "The Rugged Individualist." The apartment building was wet and sandy but structurally undamaged. My landlady arranged to have it cleaned within a couple of days. She also decided to leave the electricity on for a little while to help dry the structure out, giving me access to electricity for a month.

The motel where I worked was not so lucky. It sustained major damage and closed for the winter while being rebuilt. I was now without a job.

Not long after the storm, I awoke one morning and was unable to walk. Once again, my legs were in terrible pain. I assumed it was a delayed muscle reaction from the strain I put myself through during the storm. The next day the pain got much worse and I got scared. One of my friends took me to the hospital.

I stayed for three days in the ward while they ran tests—they suspected polio. I hated being there. I felt helpless and that my life was totally out of my control. There was some concern among the staff about how I was going to pay for everything. Dorothy couldn't be found, and the doctors had the same difficulty getting to Isadore through wife #2 as I had had. Luckily for me, the doctors felt that they couldn't toss me out until they found what was wrong.

As it turned out, I had arthritis. I could go home with medicine (which they gave me), rest, and within a week or so, the pain would lessen and I could resume my normal activities.

My legs did get better as promised, but I soon found that living on the ocean was not the best thing for arthritis. After the pills ran out, I didn't have the money to refill the prescription. I learned to live with the frequent pain for the next five years or so, and I kept quiet about the pain during my time in Ocean City for fear that it might interfere with my getting another job.

The rest of the winter—which was only getting started—was one survival test after another. I found that because of the storm damage, there would be no jobs available until spring. I would have to make my savings of around $200 last over the next six or seven months.

This meant rationing my meals. I calculated that if I ate one meal every three days, I would be able to keep that rhythm up until spring. Otherwise, I'd run out of money ahead of time and not be able to eat at all. I won't pretend it was easy. Sometimes I got so hungry I just cried. Once it got so bad, I had to knock on neighbors' doors and beg for food. I got a can of chopped kale. (I've had a soft spot in my heart for kale ever since.) A friend who had one of the few remaining coffee shop jobs periodically stole hamburgers for me. And every once in awhile, I got invited to a friend's house for dinner.

In early winter, I lost my electricity and had to spend the rest of the season in the cold while doing my homework and journal writing by candlelight.

Two or three times throughout the winter, Dorothy appeared on my doorstep. She even moved in for a few days, but I didn't encourage her to stay. I hated seeing her. I hated her drunkenness—the way she would weave through a door and bang into walls, that stale alcohol and smoke smell that permeated her clothes, and her yellow eyeballs—especially her yellow, bloodshot eyeballs. She was out of control and I was afraid of her. My existence made her angry—at me and at herself—so she would come in, express her anger by wrecking the place, and then leave.

In spring, a new place called Frontier Town opened seven miles out of town. It was a replica of an old frontier fort, and all employees had to dress up as cowboys and Indians. The Indians turned out to be authentic Native Americans who traveled around the country for just this kind of summer job. I was hired as the cowgirl in charge of the penny candy store. Several weeks after I started, I changed jobs and became the teller in the bank.

Most of the boys and men who worked there lived in the bunkhouses. There was a separate house for the marshal/manager, wife (the rodeo trick rider) and young son. His wife invited me to live with them in their house when they found out that I was losing my apartment and had no place to go. So for the summer, I was safe.

Frontier Town rendered another blow to my preconceived notions of reality. I had just come through a year of dealing with my mother, father, apartments, food (or lack thereof), money (or lack thereof), hospitals, cold, darkness, storms . . . and now I was living in a wild west fort, working in a bank, getting robbed every hour on the half hour, hustling bandits out the back window so they could escape the law, getting shot in gun fights and, in the quiet times, weighing little vials of ground-up brass nails that the kiddies got from the panning stream, and handing them wooden nickels in exchange. All this make-believe stuff became my new life. It gave me a sofa to sleep on, food and a wage.

But it wasn't a completely carefree summer for me. The strains of the past year showed as the pressure of survival lifted. I was very nervous and unsure of myself with my new family and friends. I felt as if people considered me an odd duck—and I'm sure, in some ways, I was. I was constantly afraid the people who were helping me would get tired and toss me out. So I would either not respond to them out of fear of making the wrong move, or try to do something I thought would please them and end up feeling I had only managed to get in their way. Then there were times when I had real difficulty simply pulling myself together.

I didn't see Dorothy all summer. A couple of times, I tried to get in touch with Isadore and again was put off by wife #2. Once she called just to tell me she and Isadore were getting a divorce (which wasn't true) and that it was all my fault for causing so many problems in the family. I had had enough of this woman, stopped her tirade in mid-sentence, told her something comparable to "shove it!" and then slammed the phone down and stomped back to the bank—feeling satisfied.

The new school year was fast approaching. My job would end on Labor Day, and I had to find another place to stay for the winter. My pay at Frontier Town for working from 10 A.M. to

10 P.M., six days a week, was $49 (after taxes). After expenses, I was only able to save about $150 for the winter. I found a room at a motel owned by a friend of Dorothy's who assumed he'd get the rent from her. I didn't tell him differently. Living at Frontier Town had left me out of touch with what jobs would be available for the winter, so I moved into the room and got ready for school, with the hope that I could find something for the winter once I got back into town.

During the first week of school, another storm hit Ocean City. This time it was a full-blown hurricane.

Most of the city was evacuated, but my motel had a reputation for being built sturdily enough to withstand any storm. So I stayed. I watched the first half of the storm from my picture window and then took a walk around the area during the eye of the storm. The sun was out, there was no wind, the air was dry, there was a calm but eerie quiet. . . . The damage around me was all there was to indicate that we were in the midst of a disaster. As the winds began to pick up again, I returned to my room for the second half. In the bay just outside my window, I watched a fifty-foot yacht sink.

The motel had no damage, fully living up to its reputation. But the rest of the city was a mess, and any chance I might have had for getting a winter job got washed away with the storm. (If I had been smart, I would have apprenticed myself as a construction worker and had guaranteed winter work!)

The prospect of spending another winter eating once every three days depressed me. The first year, I didn't have a clue as to what those conditions would do to me. As I approached the second winter, I knew full well what hunger felt like. Also, the wife of my new landlord discovered that her husband was having an affair with Dorothy and was pressuring him to toss me out of the motel. Without money, all I'd be able to find would be another unheated, unlit place—if I was lucky.

Exhausted and depressed, I felt the walls closing in on me once again.

I don't know what made me think of it, but I remembered one of my employers at Frontier Town telling me that his daughter went to a good, Catholic girls' academy in Pennsylvania. I knew nothing about private schools or Catholic schools, but somehow I knew that if I could get into this place, I'd be safe. I called the man to get the name and address of the school, and he offered to call them for me and set up an appointment with Admissions. He called back that day to tell me the nuns would see me and my mother the following week. (What he did not tell me was that admissions to the school had been closed for the year, and he had to push hard to get them to see me.)

It took me several days to track down Dorothy and several more days to convince her to come with me to Pennsylvania. On the day of our trip, she showed up drunk, leaving me no alternative but to drive. (Two years before the divorce, in one of her infrequent flashes of wisdom, Dorothy had taught me to drive. She figured it might be a handy tool for me to have.) We set out for Pennsylvania, the kid behind the wheel and the mother trying her bleary best to read the road map.

It wasn't that Dorothy didn't care about my going to the academy. She got drunk that day because she was nervous about presenting herself to a bunch of nuns. She honestly didn't want to blow my chances. There was a side of her that knew I was in trouble and that she should be helping me. And every once in a while, her desire for me to be happy and not experience pain

33

would slip right up on her, and she'd act out of concern for me. Going to Pennsylvania was one of those times. So to calm her nerves, to bolster the bravery needed to meet the nuns, she drank a boatload of booze.

Just as we pulled into the academy driveway, Dorothy passed out. By this time, nothing was going to get in the way of my getting into the academy. I pushed her over onto the seat and parked the car so that no one could see her. Then I went in for my appointment.

I made up another one of my crazy stories—something about my mother becoming ill and walking to a drug store in the village to get some aspirin. She would be joining us as soon as she could. But she hoped we wouldn't mind getting started without her so that their time wouldn't be wasted. (My ex-employer had already told the nuns about Dorothy, and they suspected what was really going on.) Without missing a beat, they went right into the interview.

The school sounded like everything I could ever possibly want. At least, it was everything I needed at that moment. I was totally smitten by the kindness of the nuns during the interview. I had read *The Nun's Story,* so I *knew* nuns were good, kind, loving, gentle . . . your basic, all-around, perfect women dedicated to God. And these ladies were proving it.

When asked who would be paying my tuition (which was about $2500 yearly), I told them my father would. At the time, I had no idea how I would get him to pay that tuition, but this was something I could deal with later.

I was taken on a tour of the school, introduced to some of my future classmates, measured for uniforms and told to report back in two weeks. It wasn't until I felt secure about having been admitted that I told the nuns I wasn't Catholic. (I didn't dare tell them I was Jewish.) To my relief, they told me it didn't matter, that about 25 percent of the girls were non-Catholic. I would not have to take any of the religion classes, but I would be expected to join the girls for Mass on Sundays.

Dorothy "came to" during the trip back to Maryland. I was furious at her and didn't talk to her for the rest of the trip.

For the next two weeks, I continued going to classes at my old school and managed to keep from being thrown out of the motel by promising faithfully that I would be leaving permanently in two weeks anyway. I didn't have to worry about packing my things until the last minute. Since arriving in Ocean City, my possessions had dwindled dramatically.

Dorothy promised she would drive me to the academy, and, lo and behold, she showed up more sober than I had seen her in a long time.

Together, we left for Pennsylvania.

The academy was situated in a small village near Hanover, Pennsylvania, and housed about eighty girls, grades one through twelve. The school itself, over one hundred years old, was run by the American offshoot of a French order of nuns. They also ran a small, exclusive girls' college in Philadelphia that had a reputation for quality. The college was their major source of pride, and it was where the younger nuns at the academy aimed to teach. The older nuns had already put in their time at the college and were assigned to the academy so that they could ease into retirement.

There were two old brick buildings on the grounds. The smaller one contained the dormitory and classrooms for grades one through eight. The larger one contained the chapel, student dining room and separate dormitories for each of the high school grades—plus three small private rooms and a double room for the exclusive use of senior class members. Off the large dining room was a wing containing the nuns' dining room and their private sleeping quarters. That area had a mysterious, forbidden air about it since the nuns were very strict about not permitting any student to enter. (At first, I thought it was because we mere mortals weren't supposed to see them eat.)

When I arrived in November 1961, the junior class dorm was filled to capacity. I was given one of the two remaining empty private rooms and told that my good fortune was because I was non-Catholic, and they didn't want me to be disturbed on weekday mornings when the girls in the dormitory got up early to go to Mass.

The room was tiny, with a high ceiling. It contained a single bed, a vanity with a lamp, one chair and a closet. It also had electricity and heat, but thanks to the window, I never had to worry about the room overheating. On cold, windy nights, I had a direct reminder of what I had left behind in Ocean City. On snowy nights, I could lie in bed and watch the flakes that were blowing through the cracks in the closed window collect on the sill in little drifts. Despite this, I loved my room. It gave me the sense of being in a little, protected nest. It didn't matter what horrors occurred in the outside world. I had the safety and security of my nest.

The nun in charge of the junior class was Sister Mary Agnes —or SMA. She was young, typically overweight, rather warm and jolly. The girls in my class liked her—that said a lot for her. Because she was the prefect of our class, she lived in a tiny room (cell) just outside the junior dormitory and up the hall from me. Her presence was calculated to keep us young ladies in line.

SMA took a liking to me and would come into my room at night to talk. Mostly, she encouraged me to talk. I valued her friendship, and not long after arriving at the academy, I told her the story about the trouble I was having with my parents. She asked my permission to relate it to Mother Superior and assured me that they would help me with the situation. I had nothing to worry about any longer, she said—all I had to do was concentrate on my studies. Relieved, I dropped the problem in her ample lap and focused on learning the routine of the school.

From the first Sunday I went to Mass, I became enchanted by the mystery and movement of that ritual. Bells rang. Everyone stood, knelt and genuflected in a synchronized choreography. The priest went through his dance in front of the alter while saying Latin prayers. Nuns and students responded in Latin. Colorful vestments, lighted candles, linen, gold, crystal . . . the makings of a true magical mystery tour.

I left that first Mass determined that I was going to learn how to breeze through this thing as casually as everyone else in the chapel. For this, I would need to go to more Masses. But the thing that finally motivated me to get out of bed at 4:50 A.M. for daily Mass had nothing to do with my well-intentioned desire to learn. It was Sister Edward Eileen and her cowbell.

Eddie was the high school math and science teacher. She was also prefect of the freshman class and lived in a "cell" near the freshman dormitory, down the hall from us. She was young, intense, serious . . . and had a nasty streak in her that sometimes made her a bit sadistic toward the students, especially upper classmen, since she tended to be protective toward the freshmen who she saw as underdogs. She had one job in the dormitories. Every morning after Mass, she would make the rounds, and, after flipping the overhead light switches, she would clang a rather large cowbell and yell *"Benedicamus Domino,"* to which the girls were to reply *"Deo Gratias"* and kneel by their beds, waiting for the start of morning prayers. (I can't repeat what the girls really muttered under their breath in response to Eddie's *"Benedicamus Domino."*) As if this weren't enough, if one of the girls was slow about getting out of bed, ol' Eddie would stand over her and continuously clang that cowbell until she was kneeling on the ice-cold linoleum floor. The only way I could stop this woman from putting me through that ridiculous routine was by getting up every morning for Mass, thus showing her that I was already up, with prayers said, and dressed.

Daily Mass was quite different from Sunday Mass. First of all, I arrived at the chapel the first morning to find that I was the only student attending. It must have been wishful thinking when I was told I could have a private room so that I wouldn't be disturbed by all the other girls getting up for daily Mass. (I was given the same room in my senior year and told it was so I wouldn't disturb the other girls when *I* got up for Mass.) Secondly, there were about fifty-five nuns living in the convent, and on Sundays they sat side by side in the back pews—the students sitting in the front pews. On weekdays, they sat in a pattern, spreading themselves throughout the entire chapel. It was a pattern that never changed during all the time I was there. When I showed up, one of the nuns told me where to sit, and I became part of the pattern. Also, what took the priest forty minutes to say on Sundays only took him seventeen minutes to say on weekdays. My state of total confusion on Sundays was magnified ten-fold on weekdays. But in six weeks, I was able to fly through any Mass flawlessly.

Not long after my arrival, SMA told me that my father was coming to the academy to visit me. She apparently was taking care of my problems.

He arrived on a Friday evening with wife #2. A nun escorted them into the private guest living room and then sent SMA to get me. On my way there, she kept telling me that everything was okay and that my troubles were finally over.

At first, just he and I spoke. We were both very tight—it felt more like a business meeting between strangers. He asked how I liked the school. I said fine. He asked if the nuns were okay. I said yes. Were the classes okay? Yes. A few more minutes of the same type of questions and answers. Then there was silence. He broke the silence by saying that eventually, when things got settled, he still wanted me to live with him and for us to be a family.

That's when wife #2 chimed in. She began screaming, literally screaming, that I would be allowed in *her* home over her dead body. I was a conniving, spoiled brat who wanted to break up their marriage. I was the real cause of the problems in the mar-riage. . . . Her face got red as she ranted on. I didn't know what to do except sit there and look at her. Isadore tried to calm her down, but she pushed his efforts aside, saying that he let me rule him. She got up, announced to him that she would meet him in the car and stormed out of the room, slamming the door.

Isadore, noticeably confused, muttered something about com-ing back soon to finish our discussion. Then he left. No "Good-bye." No kiss. No "Do you need anything?" He just left.

SMA had been sitting in the office across the hall, eavesdropping. I was still sitting in the living room trying to figure out what had just happened when she came in. She told me to go to my room, that I was not to worry. She and Mother Superior would deal with my father.

A couple of weeks later, they came again. I met them in the living room and we went through the same routine. First, the stiff calm. But as soon as he got around to my living with them, the wife started screaming. This time I tried to stop her by telling Isadore the trouble I had been having with her for the past year and a half. That was a mistake. That's when he changed on me. He would hear no criticism about his wife—especially from a *child*. His still-blue eyes locked into mine as he shouted that if I didn't change my attitude, if I didn't straighten up and start living my life "properly," I would get nothing from him.

While this was going on, I could clearly feel myself split. The "inside me" had withdrawn and was looking down on the situation as an outside observer, whispering wisecrack commentary in my head on the absurdities Isadore was yelling. The "other me" was sitting there in the room in shock, absorbing the verbal pounding that was coming at me. My "inside self" felt that this was just an experience, albeit a difficult experience—that, like a storm, I only had to wait it out. My "outside self" was terrified.

He kept yelling and yelling. I was sure he was going to hit me. Instead, he told me not to bother calling him until I decided to change my lousy attitude. (Always, it was my lousy attitude.)

They left together this time.

SMA came into the room again. I was to go to my room and not worry about anything. She and Mother Superior would handle my father.

The Christmas vacation was fast approaching and I needed a place to stay. The nuns would not let me go to Ocean City unless they knew for sure that my mother would be there for me. Dorothy had not contacted me at all since my coming to the academy, and they were having no luck in finding her. So they decided to try Isadore again. After all, I needed some place to go for Christmas.

The third meeting was almost a replay of the first and second meetings. The stiff calm . . . then the screaming, the accusations. Finally they stormed out.

I sat there for awhile, totally stunned. SMA didn't come. Knowing the routine by now, I headed up the stairs to my room. I was walking through the corridor outside the junior class dormitory when a classmate passed me and cheerfully asked how the visit with my father had gone.

I don't know what happened at that point. When I became aware again, I was lying on one of the beds in the dormitory. One of my classmates was sitting on top of me, slapping me in the face. I could tell she was hitting me hard by the power of her arm, but I couldn't feel anything. I could hear myself screaming but I couldn't feel myself scream. The girl who had asked me the original, innocent question was standing next to me trying to pin my arms down. Normally, she had a lovely light brown, South American complexion. I remember looking up at her from the bed and seeing her face drained, pale white and terrified. I was struck by how strange she looked with a pale complexion. I saw SMA rush into the room. She slapped me in the face and shook me wildly by the shoulders. I stopped screaming. She told the girls to stay with me, that she'd be right back, and rushed out of the dormitory. She told me later that she had gone outside to try to stop my father before he left. (She didn't realize he had long since gone.) I think that if she had gotten hold of him that night, she would have beaten him to a bloody pulp. Bride of Christ or not, she was going to get him.

By the time she came back, I was quietly sitting on the bed with the others attentively staring at me, ready to jump into action if I should "go crazy" again. SMA told me to take my shower and get ready for bed. Then she brought me a cup of tea and told me, once again, not to worry about anything.

The next day, I attended Mass and classes as usual. I was numb and quiet, and grateful just to drift through the well-defined routine at the academy.

After lunch SMA told me that she had talked to one of the parish priests about my situation and that he had offered to talk to me. She suggested that I think about it. She didn't want to push me, but she honestly felt I needed more help and this man could possibly give it to me. If, after seeing him one time, I wanted to see him again, she would arrange for me to have permission to leave the school grounds as often as was necessary.

I didn't have to think about it—I knew I needed help.

That afternoon, I walked the three blocks to the rectory and met Father Lahout. We spent three hours together. Mostly, I talked and he listened. By the time the three hours were over, he had even managed to make me laugh. For the rest of the school year, I met with Father Lahout an average of three times a week.

This amazing man gave me several important ingredients that I needed for the inner journey I was moving through. You see, it was truly an inner journey, even though outwardly it appeared that I was being reduced to dealing with an endless stream of external distractions. But these distractions—admittedly *major* distractions—were designed to blow away old expectations that had functioned in me as limitations. I had already been through a year and a half of concentrated inner chipping away, breaking up and breaking down. Through my relationship with this priest, I began a process of healing and rebuilding.

Father Lahout was a man in his mid-thirties, one of six children raised by immigrant parents. They were the classic example of a family held together with a mix of love, discipline and religion. I was able to benefit from this through my relationship with Father Lahout. From the beginning, he displayed an ease and warmth toward me. By then, my instincts had sharpened, and it was easier for me to spot phonies. Although I didn't have much experience with people like him, I could still tell that his openness, ease and caring were genuine.

He *listened* to me. Part of my problem up to that point had been people's simple belief that since I was just a kid, it was most unlikely that I was telling the truth about my parents— therefore, I didn't need help. With Father Lahout, I didn't have that problem.

I don't want to give the impression that our relationship gave me magical, instant inner strength, self-worth and self-esteem. It took a long time for him to break through my defenses—which ultimately enabled him to provide me with an environment for my healing. It was the *start* of my rebuilding and strengthening process.

The subject of religion was not a major issue between us. He wasn't the type to notch his belt with the conquest of another convert. In fact, he rather enjoyed my Jewish background. But religion aside, he didn't hesitate to share with me his personal code of moral beliefs. And he felt particularly strong about the commandment to "Honor thy father and thy mother." He firmly believed that my parents were as crazy as could be—but despite that, they were my parents and I had to deal with them. I could not simply walk away from them.

As I had no idea where my mother was, Isadore became the only parent we worked on. Father Lahout encouraged me to write letters to my father, explaining how I felt about being on my own so much, how I hoped we could become a family and that I loved him. (Truth was, I didn't think I loved him. I thought that possibly, if I said it enough, maybe I would come to love him.) I wrote lengthy letters, spilling my heart and guts out all over the place, then gave the letters to Father Lahout to be checked before mailing, just to make sure I didn't write anything unintentionally stupid that might cause an argument.

The letters were either returned unopened or opened and mailed back in another envelope with a letter from wife #2 telling me that my father didn't wish to speak to me. One letter did reach Isadore. I got a note from him saying he didn't know who was coaching me to write these things, but he wasn't impressed and I still had to change my lousy attitude.

The responses even got Father Lahout angry. Wife #2 was beyond his comprehension and was reduced to an irrational obstacle to be worked around. But I still couldn't turn my back on my father. I still had to try.

I had spent the Christmas vacation with one of my classmates and was preparing to do something similar at Easter when suddenly I got word from SMA that Isadore wanted me to spend the vacation with him in Baltimore. Although Father Lahout saw it as an opportunity to break the ice between us, he wasn't stupid. Something inside told him to set up an escape for me in case something drastic happened in Baltimore. He found that Isadore's new apartment was just across the street from Loyola College. So he gave me a letter and said if I needed help in Baltimore, I was to walk across the street to the college, ask for this priest (a friend of his) and give him the letter.

I arrived in Baltimore to find that Isadore was away on a business trip and would not be back for two days. The idea of being alone with the wife petrified me. But she treated me politely, sometimes even kindly. I relaxed a little, she relaxed a little, and, before we knew it, things became enjoyable.

During our second evening together, she confided to me how difficult the marriage was for her, how hard it was to live with Isadore. I sat and listened to her until 2 A.M. She said cruel things about him, but because of my own experience with him, I could only sympathize. She also told me it was Isadore who didn't want me living with them, not her, and that she was working on him to let me live with them the coming summer. I could have my own room, we would have fun decorating it, etc., etc.

The next day Isadore returned. It was Thursday and I had gone to the cathedral down the street to see my first Holy Thursday Mass. By the time I got back, the atmosphere in the apartment had shifted dramatically. I walked into the den after saying hello to everyone. Isadore followed me in, slamming the door. He was enraged—totally enraged. It didn't take me long to figure out from his rantings and ravings that wife #2 had repeated the entire conversation from the evening before, but rather than tell him that she had said those things about him, she told him I said them.

I think if it had not been against the law, he would have killed me. Instead, he kicked me out of the apartment. He didn't care where I went or how I got there; I just had to get out as soon as I got my things packed.

A student answered the main door at Loyola. I asked for the man whose name was on the envelope of Father Lahout's letter. About fifteen minutes later, a priest with a puzzled look on his face appeared and introduced himself. I opened my mouth to explain why I was there but started to cry instead. So I just gave him the letter and continued to cry while he read it. Apparently, Father Lahout had been quite thorough in his explanations. After reading the letter, the priest took charge of the situation.

The first problem was to find a place for me to go for the rest of the vacation. I had a list of several classmates' addresses and phone numbers, and he called until he found a family to take me in. Then he got the bus connections, gave me money for the ticket and the trip and, in about two hours, was seeing me off at the Trailways Bus Station.

I arrived in Dover, Delaware, in the late evening hours. I remember the irony of walking through my classmate's front door and hearing a bunch of door chimes sounding out the tune to "Bless This House." The priest had called after I was on the bus to let them know my arrival time and the condition I might be in because of the situation in Baltimore. By the time I got to Dover, my classmate, her sister and mother welcomed me with sympathetic, open arms.

The option of visiting Isadore in his home was no longer viable—even in Father Lahout's mind. He conceded that the man was impossible—the wife even more so—and the best I could do now was to avoid giving them further opportunity to hurt me. But that still didn't mean to Father Lahout that I could emotionally turn my back on Isadore. Someday things could change.

For the remainder of the school year, I continued to see Father Lahout three times a week. We'd sit there eating ice cream, talking about the crazy things that went on at the academy, the trouble the nuns were having with some of the girls, the trouble the girls were having with some of the nuns, his family, his old seminary days, the history of languages (his hobby), surviving (my hobby), and my feelings about my parents and what was happening to me. From him, I began to get the idea that I could have a sense of inner calm, inner stability, even peace—no matter how chaotic the environment around me became.

One thing happened at the academy at the very end of my junior year that was to significantly alter the course of my senior year.

It was customary for the outgoing senior class to nominate the candidates for the next year's president of student council. (The internal politics of what happened get complex, but I'll push on.) There was a girl in my class who had been groomed by the nuns since her freshman year for this prestigious post. The scuttlebutt about her was that her father had donated the furniture for an entire dormitory when she was a freshman, and it was this act of extravagance that brought her to the minds and hearts of the nuns early on. She was ideally suited for the role—beautiful, well-heeled, with excellent grades and a trained singing voice that got her the top singing assignments in school. She was the absolute model of who the nuns wanted to have represent the academy. What they didn't know was that she was dishonest, drank gin out of a shampoo bottle, was into some serious fooling around with a number of boys and hated the academy, the nuns and the Catholic religion. The outgoing senior class knew this and banded together to keep her from being nominated.

The rest of the tradition in this passing of power was for the high school students to vote on the nominees at the same assembly, immediately after the nominations. There was no campaigning—no posters, no promises, no speeches.

Out of the seniors' conspiracy, there were only three nominations—none of which included this particular girl, one of which included me. I later learned that the seniors had fixed the election with the sophomores, thus assuring my victory. Not knowing any of this, I was stunned.

The senior class prefect, ol' Virgo Regina, was also the prefect of the student council. She, in particular, had been waiting for the day when this girl would become president. She was sure they would make one great team. Instead, she was now faced with the prospect of working with an interloper. She did not take the election very gracefully. She got up during my acceptance speech, told me to sit down and then announced that starting next year, no one could be nominated for president of student council unless she had been a student at the academy for two full years at the time of nomination. She had clearly set the tone for my senior year.

Just as I was about to panic about where I was going for the summer, Dorothy popped up. Her classic timing again. She was now living in Riverdale, Maryland, and had a new apartment ready for me. Since I had no other offers, I had to go to Riverdale.

Two weeks before school ended, Mother Superior called me to her office. It seemed that Isadore had not paid anything toward my tuition, and if the problem couldn't be solved before school ended, I would not be allowed to return the next year. She wanted me to talk to the academy lawyer about the situation. Perhaps he could come up with a solution.

The result of the meeting with the lawyer was a letter—sent to Isadore on my behalf, threatening to sue him for non-support of a minor. (We discovered that the court had awarded him custody of me at the divorce.) Within a couple of days, a check for the full amount of the tuition was received by the lawyer. Mother Superior gave me the glad news and told me I was now promoted out of the eleventh grade and accepted back for next year.

The day after the senior class graduated, I packed and, with suitcase, picture and record player in hand, headed for Riverdale, a suburb of Washington, D.C.

To say that I was not exactly thrilled with the prospect of spending the summer with Dorothy would be an understatement. I feared the woman and her drinking. Because of my experiences in Ocean City, I wasn't nearly as stressed about the food and shelter issue. I assumed I could get a job that would keep me in food for the summer and, hopefully, have enough left over to finance my senior year expenses. Neither parent gave me money for school expenses and, although I had $30 left over from the $75 I had when I had arrived at the academy, I was sure this wouldn't cover my senior year.

One of Dorothy's lady friends met me at the bus station. During the conversation on the way to see my mother at her new place of employment, I learned that she was telling people that she had been in constant contact with me at the academy, had wanted to visit me but I wouldn't see her, had sent me money and gifts but I never wrote or contacted her to say thank you. In essence, Dorothy had built a fantasy about her relationship with me, and I soon learned that everyone around her had bought her story. By the time I arrived on the scene, Dorothy's friends considered me a rotten ingrate of a daughter who was taking advantage of this poor woman who was working her tush off keeping both of our lives together.

She had moved to Riverdale to start a new life. Why she chose Riverdale, I don't know. She rented a nice one-bedroom apartment, bought a new car (through a deal with one of her new friends) and got a new job—as a bartender.

Her working nights left me alone in the apartment from early afternoon—she liked to arrive at the bar early to help set up for the evening (so she said)—until around three or four in the morning, when she would stumble in, totally smashed. She'd collapse on the bed, sleep it off until late the next morning and then start the routine over. Except for two or three hours in late morning, I didn't have to deal with her directly.

A couple of weeks after I arrived, she stopped coming home, staying away for weeks at a time. I solved my food problem by taking $20 from her wallet every time she showed up. I could make that stretch for three weeks, if necessary, by loading up on cereal and spaghetti. I discovered that I could get two full meals out of a pound of spaghetti noodles (16 cents) topped with a can of tomato soup (8 cents)—not necessarily a healthy diet, but a filling one.

Riverdale was a suburban community, not a resort town, and although it offered some summer jobs, they were taken by the time I arrived in mid-June. So I had to content myself with staying in the apartment.

I developed a daily rhythm of reading, writing, cleaning, walking and watching television—a gentle rhythm broken only when Dorothy arrived on the scene. There would be a flurry of activity with her yelling at me, banging doors and cabinets until it was a miracle that they were still on their hinges, making messes throughout the apartment and dropping a bunch of dirty clothes that she exchanged for clean ones. Then she'd leave again.

The tension of never knowing when Dorothy was going to blow through wore me down. Pretty soon, I couldn't eat without feeling as if I was about to vomit any minute. I found a doctor in the area (whose bill I charged to Dorothy), and he informed me that I had a spastic colon—a poor man's ulcer. The very first thing he asked me was whether either one of my parents had a drinking problem. When I said yes, he told me that he had seen a number of teenagers with spastic colons and all had a parent with drinking problems. He gave me some pills and sent me on my way with the advice that I needed to learn to relax.

The spastic colon was a blessing in disguise. My life had become so intense by this time that I had difficulty knowing when I was in emotional pain. In order to survive, I had separated many of my emotions from my situation. If something scared me, it didn't matter. I still had to deal with it, and I didn't have time to waste dealing with the fear. The spastic colon, which was activated when I reached a certain level of tension, kept me from emotionally closing down by calling my attention to the things that were seriously hurting me.

In late July, I decided to convert to Catholicism—just like that.

I found the nearest rectory and presented myself to a priest for instructions. In the course of trying to find out who I was and where I came from, the priest began to suspect that I might be in an unusual situation. I told him about my being in Riverdale, about my mother, about her drinking. He immediately latched onto Dorothy's drinking, suggested she might be an alcoholic (the first time I had heard the word "alcoholic" used in reference to Dorothy) and said he knew some people who might be able to help me. Would I mind if he sent someone to talk to me?

A woman arrived at my door that evening, explaining that she was the wife of an alcoholic and belonged to a group called Al-Anon, a division of Alcoholics Anonymous. She also explained that there was another division of AA called Alateen, for the teenage children of alcoholics, and that she felt they could help me. The kids were meeting that night, and she would be glad to take me to the meeting and bring me back home. As she spoke, I could feel the compassion and understanding that this woman had for what I was going through with Dorothy.

That night I went to my first Alateen meeting.

There were about twenty-five kids at the meeting who opened themselves to me immediately. Their first concerns had to do with my immediate living situation and whether I was in need—food, clothes, different shelter, protection from the alcoholic parent. We decided that I needed companionship and food. So for the next seven weeks, until I went back to the academy, I was visited often, and all visitors came bearing groceries. I was included in group outings, taken to the movies and, of course, always given a ride to the meetings.

My adult sponsor, who had been sober for twelve years, went to the bar where Dorothy worked and, over several ginger ales, observed her, coming away with the conclusion that she was indeed an alcoholic.

That news relieved me. Dorothy wasn't just a drunk, she was an alcoholic. My sessions with Alateen were quickly teaching me the difference. I learned about the disease—how it affected the drinker. Dorothy's unpredictable behavior suddenly became predictable. I read books and pamphlets that treated alcoholism as a disease and found that her behavior fit right in with the recognized symptoms and patterns.

From the kids, I was learning that the feelings I had toward her, which I felt were shameful for any respectable child to feel toward a mother, were natural and shared at some time by everyone in the group. The anger, the shame, the disgust, the hate, the fear—it was all expected under the circumstances, and it was okay.

The more I learned about alcoholic behavior and about my own personal pitfalls and patterns of reacting to that behavior, the more I was able to protect and stabilize myself and keep from being emotionally swept into Dorothy's life as she stumbled and crashed through mine.

It wasn't an easy order for any of us to achieve. We were all hurting. A couple of the kids who so feared being alcoholics themselves began to drink to disprove it, got into trouble and ended up needing to go to the meetings for alcoholics. One thirteen-year-old girl came to the meetings faithfully but would never say a word. At first, we passed it off as shyness. Eventually, she opened up and we found out it was pure terror that kept her silent. It seems that her alcoholic father would rape her every time he got drunk. We got her placed into another home immediately.

We were a tight, supportive group who would jump to the aid of another if we even suspected foul play. At last I found friends who understood what I was dealing with. Before, I had been trying to explain my situation to friends who came from stable homes. They simply couldn't understand what I was saying. It didn't figure in their concept of reality. With the kids from Alateen, my problems were very familiar. They didn't go into a frenzy if I called to say that Dorothy had wrecked the apartment and was now passed out in the bathtub. They'd just come over, encourage me to pull the plug in the tub so she wouldn't drown and then take me to their home for the night. They'd even help clean up the mess when I went back.

I had just weeks to learn as much as possible before going back to school. During that period, we organized and hosted the first Eastern Seaboard Alateen Conference. We had over a hundred teenagers from Boston to North Carolina for three days of discussions on living with the alcoholic parent and on problems in setting up Alateen groups. It was such a success that the conference became an annual event hosted by a different group each year.

Through Alateen, I began to identify and order my emotions, and to develop a sense of inner power that allowed me to move through life not as a victim who constantly reacted to the destructive actions of others, but more as a creative individual who continued moving through life *despite* the actions of others around me. I was learning that the power center that motivated my life did not exist outside of me, nor was the power held by anyone around me. It was inside me, and no one could diminish its potency unless I allowed them to.

In mid-September, I arrived back at the academy with my sponsor and a carload of kids from my group. The nuns were gracious as I showed them around, until they learned where my friends came from. The nuns were not at all happy about my cavorting with the low life—and anything connected with a bunch of alcoholics was definitely low life.

My senior year came right out of *One Flew Over the Cuckoo's Nest*. I don't know what happened over the summer but, by the time school started, all the nuns associated with the high school were operating with a high count of loose screws. To make matters worse, SMA had been transferred over the summer to another school. I had lost my friend and ally.

Virgo Regina was still angry about my being elected president of student council and quickly established a pattern of revenge toward me. Unfortunately, she was not only prefect of student council. She was also prefect of the senior class, our homeroom teacher and the new resident along the senior class dormitory corridor. We were rarely without her, and I could barely escape her.

From the first week, Virgo started chipping away at me. She would give me a list of duties to perform as student council president—dumb stuff, such as checking the dormitories after the final morning bell to make sure no one was hiding out, and then reversing herself so that it looked as if I was guilty of breaking the very academy rules I was supposed to be enforcing. I would carry out the various duties she gave me—all of which would necessitate my showing up five minutes late for homeroom—and she would go into a blood-curdling tirade about the horrible example I was setting for the other students. The entire high school could hear her yelling at me. The woman truly resented me, and there was nothing I could do to change her feelings.

One morning after a particularly outrageous and loud dressing down that Virgo brought to a dramatic end by storming out of the classroom, my classmates convened a meeting to discuss what was happening to me. They agreed that Virgo was acting unfairly and decided they would protect me from her distorted games by warning me when they saw her in action. So for the rest of the year, I was warned when Virgo was "at it again"—which drove her nuts because she couldn't figure out how I was avoiding her traps.

There was nothing I could personally do about Virgo. There was a rule at the academy that prohibited any student from making a negative remark or complaint of any kind about a nun to another student or nun. If we had any complaints, we had to go to the nun involved. Also, Virgo was a nun with power. She was in the Number Two spot, right behind Mother Superior. I don't know if she had been elected to this position or if it was based on her age (which was fast approaching ancient) or tenure as a teacher. However she got the position, she was given great deference and respect by the other nuns.

It didn't help matters that I had to work with her on the student council. I entered my year as president thinking that this council, as with most councils in other schools, would function as the representative student body to the faculty. In fact, the academy student council was the representative of the faculty to the students. We were expected to do a lot of the nuns' dirty work, especially when it came to student discipline. The focus of the council centered around rules and detention slips—*lots* of detention slips.

The rules were numerous. No talking on the stairs or in the halls. No sassing nuns—to be enforced at the nuns' discretion. If two students from different grades arrived at a closed door at the same time, the student from the lower grade had to hold the door open for the upper classmen. *All* students had to hold all doors for any nun. Each girl's uniform had to touch the floor when she knelt. If it was too short, the hem was ripped out and she was thrown into detention for a few days. . . .

We really weren't a student council—we were an SS troop for the nuns. Every time I brought up suggestions to make the council more student-oriented, Virgo told me I was too new at the academy to understand or respect its traditions.

I was also responsible (as student council president) for the morals of all the girls in the high school. If a girl got pregnant—which happened twice that year—I had to go before Mother Superior and explain how and why it happened. Then I had to convince her that it was impossible for me to have personally stopped the dastardly deed. I was equally responsible for the girls' smoking and drinking habits—habits that young, refined Catholic ladies were not supposed to have. Since I was quickly able to face the undeniable fact that there was no way I was going to be able to stop the majority of my classmates from debauching their way through their senior year, I decided to put my effort into keeping the nuns from discovering any of the girls' little indiscretions. Except pregnancy. That I couldn't cover up.

It took every ounce of creativity in me to cover for these girls for an entire year. We would come back to the academy after being bused to a dance at a local school, and half the girls would be drunk. My job was to keep the nun who was waiting for us at the door occupied while those who were too drunk to walk were carried past her to the dorm. I'd stand there like an idiot telling her about the *wonderful* time we all had at the dance, how terrific the music was and how well the boys could dance . . . on and on until the last girl was dragged by.

I managed to keep the drinking sprees a secret until two days before graduation. The priests at the other school found out about the dance activities from one of the boys—who apparently was caught drunk in his dorm and decided to save his own neck by implicating others. Virgo was phoned, and all hell started flying everywhere. After countless discussions between Virgo and Mother Superior, it was decided that for the sake of the parents, graduation exercises would not be called off.

Virgo wasn't the only nun gone mad that year. There was Charlie, whose madness was more cute than destructive. She taught sophomore religion, Latin and English—and to the seniors, typing. The scuttlebutt surrounding Charlie was that she had been a legal secretary before entering the convent. We embellished the rumors by suggesting that Charlie had driven her boss so crazy that he forced her into the convent just to get her out of his hair.

Talking to her was like suddenly slipping into another time zone and finding oneself in a George Burns–Gracie Allen routine. One winter evening I was trying to convince her that I needed another blanket. It was a bitter night—snowy and windy. I took her to my room and showed her the little snow drifts piling up on the inside of my window sill. I said, "See. It's *cold* in here. There's snow on my window sill. I need another blanket." She looked at me as straight as could be and said, "Of course there's snow on your window sill. It's snowing outside." Then she left. (Say "good night, Gracie.")

There was also Eddie Eileen who was destructively mad and acted it out by taking on the whole senior class. She hated the fact that her freshmen had to give deference to the seniors, especially the seniors who she decided didn't deserve respect from anyone—including the freshmen. So she set out on her own campaign. Of course, she continued the cowbell routine in the dormitories—especially the senior dormitory. (I continued going to daily Mass.) We caught her numerous times waiting at closed doors for a senior to come by, just so we could open it for her. Once the girls retaliated by removing the plumbing panel from outside the nuns' bathroom and hammering on the underside of the tub while she was taking a bath, scaring her half out of whatever was left of her wits. By the time she was able to get her gear on and come crashing out of the bathroom, the girls had replaced the panel and returned to their dormitories. Nobody knew anything about the incident—of course.

As the first semester wore on, Eddie grew more and more strange. She taught senior trigonometry, and one morning three girls showed up without having done their homework. Eddie announced that she was not going to waste her valuable time teaching a bunch of unruly ingrates and walked out of the class, never to return that entire year. Now, we had to know trig in order to graduate. We asked Virgo to intercede with Eddie for us, but she would not interfere. So, we took over our own class and spent the rest of the year teaching ourselves trigonometry. (We all got above C on the state exam.)

As the pressure built, she started taking out her frustrations on juniors and sophomores as well, especially in the dormitories. She would press girls in the mornings—yell at them, correct them sarcastically for the slightest thing, constantly dig at them. One morning she was going after the quietest, most even-tempered junior. The nun had been at her for a couple of weeks, but this morning the girl cracked and started belting Eddie in the head. The other girls yelled for me. When I arrived, the nun was bleeding from the mouth and still being beaten. The academy rule in such situations was that the students were to get another nun immediately and not interfere in the situation. I decided to follow that rule to perfection. I *walked* down three flights of stairs, through a long corridor, into the student dining room and right to the closed doors of the convent. I took a deep breath, rushed through the doors panting as if I had just finished the three-minute mile and yelled into the convent for help. By the time I returned with a platoon of nuns, the girl had beaten quite a bit of sense into Eddie. The nun was bleeding from several places in the face, but other than that there was no real harm done. The layers and folds of the habit had softened the blows.

Of course the girl was expelled from school, effective immediately. When we said good-bye to her later that morning, she was smiling—and so were we.

For some reason, despite all the craziness, I decided again to request instructions in Catholicism. I had a gut-level instinct that the Church contained a truth, and I needed to know it. Unfortunately, I couldn't go to Father Lahout. A month after I got back to school, he was transferred to another parish some distance from the academy. (I was distressed at his leaving. I wasn't sure how I was going to make it through the year without him. I had grown to love and trust this man totally.)

The priest at the rectory who decided to give me instructions was a friend of Father Lahout and knew about the close relationship we had had. He also had little patience for the nuns' regimen and decided it would be good for me to get out of the academy more than for the required weekly visit for instructions. So, during one visit we talked about religion, and during the other two weekly visits we just talked—or ate ice cream or played basketball.

Isadore and wife #2 were back in the picture. Virgo had decided that I could not be allowed to return to Riverdale on vacations if it meant spending time with my Alateen friends. She was adamant about proper young ladies not associating with alcoholics or their kids. So she contacted Isadore and suggested that he take me for the holidays. That started another barrage of letters from wife #2 and visits from them both so they could tell me what a disaster I was.

I didn't leave the academy for any holidays that year. I spent them with the nuns—which, on the whole, they resented since it was the only time during the school year when they could be together as a convent without students. Most of the time they ignored me.

The insanity of the nuns and Isadore were driving my spastic colon crazy, but seeing the priest allowed me to talk the tension out and calm the colon down without using pills. (Lucky, since, as usual, I had no money to get this prescription refilled.)

My classmates weren't as lucky and had to create their own escapes. Some became heavy drinkers, each storing their vodka in shampoo bottles. Others used bogus college campus inspection weekends to romp and frolic with boyfriends in other towns. Other girls just held all the tension in and went into a shell.

We didn't graduate from the academy, we escaped. I almost didn't escape at all since Isadore had not paid tuition—again. I went through the same routine as the year before with the lawyer and, once again, as Isadore was being threatened with a suit for non-support of a minor, he came up with the money.

He did not come to my graduation. I sent him an invitation and a picture, which he sent back with a note saying something about my lousy attitude. Dorothy could not be found. So I sent my five invitations to my Alateen friends, who showed up in full force and cheered me on.

Virgo had one last parting shot to give me. She would not

come to the ceremony because she was so angry about finding out about the drunken dances. (She still didn't know about the shampoo bottles and the shacking up and the peep shows the girls were attending on the roof outside the senior dorm windows. They'd sit there at night smoking, watching the nuns in the convent undress.) But as we descended the stage at the end of the ceremony, there was Virgo waiting for us in the wings. She gave every graduate a hug, blessed them and wished them well. Being the tallest, I was the last one in line. She took one look at me, turned and walked away. I smiled and said, "God bless you, too, Sister."

Leaving the academy as a graduate meant that I could no longer tuck myself safely away within the academic structures. I had applied to several colleges in the hope of continuing my education and stalling for four years my entrance into the world. As bad as the academy was, it still gave me three meals a day and a room in which to sleep. With my B+ average, I felt I had a good chance of being accepted and, once I got in, I could keep suing Isadore for tuition. But the day before graduation, Virgo informed me that she had included a note in all of my applications recommending that the colleges not accept me due to "my personal problems" which, she explained to me, referred to my father and her concern that he would not pay my tuition.

This left me with the prospect of surviving on my own on a full-time basis, and I was scared. It had been well over a year since I had developed that survival edge in Ocean City. In that time, I had lost the edge.

In hindsight, I realize that I was ready to move on, and, had I tucked myself away in a college for four years, I simply would have postponed the next crucial stage. It was to prove the most difficult stage because, for the first time, I was going to have to face *myself* head on. I had to become conscious of those aspects of myself that had been crucial to my survival for over three years but which were now inappropriate and, if not overcome or disciplined, would eventually destroy me. This included my becoming overwhelmed by fear, my fine-honed ability to lie, my deep desire to be taken care of by others and my search to find security from others.

After graduation, I headed back to the suburbs of Washington, D.C. to stay with the family of one of my Alateen friends. I had idyllic visions of a quiet, stable family life away from the insanity of the nuns. At the very least, anything these people had to offer me would be better than living at the academy.

Instead, I walked into a mine field. There is absolutely no logical reason why these people offered at this particular time in their lives to have me come into their home, except to say that I had to be there. It was just as simple as that. The mother had just lost the job she had held for over twelve years due to a "needed" cost-cutting move at the plant. The alcoholic father was bobbing and weaving his way through a rather extensive drunken bender. He wasn't working at all, which gave us all lots of time to deal with him around the house. The daughter, my friend, was in bed recuperating from serious corrective leg surgery that wasn't healing well. She was in pain, depressed and then angry most of the time. She was also turning into a prima donna and making a lot of demands on anyone within earshot. There was another daughter who had a drinking problem, was married to a guy who liked to use her as a punching bag, and she was pregnant with a second child that she didn't want. She came over to the house frequently to add to the general level of tension.

My first task was to get a job. Again, I landed one on my first interview—skip-tracer and collection agent with a small Washington, D.C. collection agency, another job for which I was highly unqualified.

With a little training I became a decent skip-tracer, but once I found the culprit I bought any story he had to tell me. I was usually responsible for bringing in one or two $10 checks to the company weekly—most of the time the checks bounced. The head of the company was about to fire me when, in a panic (thus stimulating a bit of creativity), I convinced him that his office was not set up well and needed a complete house cleaning and reorganization of all files and information. He agreed. And I became the office's "girl Friday."

The boss was not overwhelmed with my initiative nearly as much as he was interested in keeping a young, female body around. He pursued, and, thinking he might be the way out of the mess I found myself living in, I accepted his pursuit.

He was everything I could have possibly wanted. Older. Thirty-six. Stable. Son of a Protestant bishop (the bishop was deceased). College educated. Even a law degree. Taught history in college while he was going to law school. Spent several years in Europe working with the foreign service. Loved classical music. Wrote poetry. And not at all coincidentally, looked a little like Isadore. We married in September.

The wedding ceremony took place in the judge's chamber during a court lunch break. It was rather convenient timing since my new husband was in the courthouse that day going through a trial—a total surprise to me. He took me to the courtroom in the morning, saying that he was on trial for something like twenty counts of telephone harassment in connection with his work as a collector. It seems that he was calling folks in the middle of the night and threatening them with bodily harm if they didn't come up with the money they owed.

When the trial broke for lunch, I asked him what was going on. He assured me that it was all a mistake and that there was nothing to worry about. I believed him. I was in love.

After a quick sandwich—our wedding reception—we went back to the courtroom. By the end of the day, he was pronounced guilty and tossed into jail. His lawyer gave me the address of his mother's home and told me to go to her.

His mother was a gracious, highly intelligent, quiet woman. She stared at me as I explained that her son was in jail and that I was his new wife. After I showed her the marriage certificate, she invited me to come live in her house, since this was where her son had been living.

I can't say we shared an instant rapport with one another. She was shy. I felt out of place. The only thing that held us together was our mutual desire to find out how we were going to get her son out of jail.

What gradually came to light was something that stunned both of us.

Her son led a double life. He used two separate names and had totally different personalities with each of the names. She and I knew the same person, the one who used the name he was given at birth. The second person was a violent man who was well known by the police. The judge had been surprisingly harsh in his ruling the day we were married because he knew the D.C. police had been anxious for years to get this man behind bars. As this other man, he had set up phony businesses in Baltimore with lawyers, signed legal papers and opened phony bank accounts locally and in San Francisco. There were warrants out for his arrest for bad checks, forgery and assault.

As the weeks went by, the picture slowly unfolded. There was no question in my mind about remaining loyal to him. He was my husband, he was in trouble, and I was going to help him out of this mess. Of course, it didn't occur to me that I had married this man because I was scared and running, and that I didn't actually love him. That out of pure fear I was choosing to believe I loved him, that I should be married to him.

Looking back, I realize that it was vital for me to learn that there was a part of me capable of being overwhelmed by fear, thus causing me to run to the nearest, most convenient exit. I could be so overcome that I could create the fantasy of love, marriage, even the notion that I could get this man out of trouble. Fear can be a constructive force within us—it motivates our moments of courage. It motivates appropriate self-protection. But it can also be a destructive force, and it was this that I was to experience and explore in a number of different ways while I dealt with this marriage.

With my husband's arrest, the collection agency folded. I had to find a new job and I had to do it quickly. A chain of fancy lumber yard/home improvement stores needed cashiers, but after the personnel testing, I was told that I was overqualified. However, they happened to have an opening for a secretary in their new home improvement department, and the job was mine as long as I passed the bonding requirements. Bonding. That meant I had to take a lie detector test.

I panicked. I figured that if they were fussy enough to require a lie detector test, they would probably not want anyone in their employ who had a husband in jail. That didn't seem fair to me. I needed that job and I knew I wasn't planning to steal their money, so I decided I would lie about my husband.

That may sound like a totally stupid move, but listen, folks, it worked. In the interview, when they asked about my husband, I made up some story about his being in Rome at the Vatican II conference as part of the American Protestant lay delegation. He'd be gone for eight months (the exact period of his jail term). Now, this story wasn't as outrageous as it now sounds. The Vatican II conference was going on in Rome at the time, and there was a Protestant lay group attending from the United States. My husband was the son of a bishop. Why wouldn't he be invited to something like that? When it came time for the machine to verify the story, I had convinced myself that it was fact and I passed the test.

Every Thursday during my lunch hour, I would visit my husband in jail. For me, it meant formalities with the guards. Signing in. Getting searched. Cold gray walls. Steel doors banging. Keys rattling. Sounds echoing. The visitors' room separated me from him by a wall. I sat on a metal chair (gray to match the other decor), looked at him through a tiny diamond-shaped window just large enough to show his face and spoke to him through a phone. When my half hour was up, a guard would bang on the back of my chair with a stick.

At first, my husband was very kind to me, very sweet. Then he started asking me to convey messages and transfer papers to business partners and lawyers, all of whom were strangers to me. Everything had to be secret. He devised codes based on characters in *The Canterbury Tales* so that he could send coded instructions to me in the mail.

The people he thought would help him were reluctant to get

involved with his mess. Each time I conveyed this to him, he got more irritated with me. Finally one Thursday he started shouting at me, telling me that he didn't want to see me again; then, to punctuate his point, he picked up his chair and slammed it against the window that separated us. Guards grabbed him. Other guards hustled me out of the room into an office where a kindly, grandfatherly guard told me that it was evident to them that my husband had been mentally deteriorating. He suggested that I get this man out of my life as soon as possible. I thanked him for his advice but dismissed it.

At Christmas, my new sister-in-law visited us. She listened intently as we brought her up to date on her brother's problems. Later that night, she came to my room to say one thing: "If you were my daughter, I'd tell you to leave this man and start your life over." The jail guard saying the same thing didn't have the impact on me that she had. She loved her brother very much. But she saw that the problems were too much for me and that her brother was probably going to drag me down.

Two weeks later, I left my mother-in-law's home and moved into a rooming house in the heart of D.C. I saw a lawyer and started divorce proceedings.

There was one small problem I had to address. As far as my boss and co-workers were concerned, I still had a husband in Rome. They were always asking how he was, when he would be coming back. I had to do something now that this man wasn't going to be in my life. So I killed him off. I called the office and told my boss that my husband had died in a car accident in Rome. I would have to fly to Rome to make arrangements for the body. He gave me two weeks off. During that time, the company newspaper ran a little sympathy note to me. By the time I returned to work, everyone knew I was a widow.

Obviously, I was quite capable of lying well. I had an entire company and a lie-detector machine believing that cock-and-bull Rome story. Lying had been a integral part of my survival since age twelve. But now, if I didn't learn to reject this "tool," this escape mechanism, as totally inappropriate and unacceptable, I would never be able to continue the spiritual journey that lay ahead of me. I have learned that truth is a complex, multi-level phenomenon. Now, I would not be able to delve into that complexity if I allowed myself to use escape hatches—lies—to get out of the difficult, uncomfortable, challenging moments frequently inherent in truth.

To achieve this, it was important that I deal with the tangled mess my lies were causing, and, thanks to my estranged/dead husband, I got the opportunity to deal with it quickly.

Eight months after we had gotten married, he was released from jail and he returned to his mother's house. He called me at the rooming house to tell me I was the cause of his present situation and that if it was the last thing he did, he would destroy me—he would kill me.

The first thing he did was get me kicked out of the rooming house by calling the landlord throughout the night, telling him he would keep calling if I wasn't evicted. I found another rooming house around the corner the day I was kicked out. Next, he went after my job by calling my boss and threatening the same thing. My boss didn't even tell me about the phone calls at first, assuming it was just some weirdo. After all, my husband was dead. Then one day, he called me into his office and played a tape of several of the calls. It was my dear, departed husband all right, making all kinds of pornographic suggestions about my moral character (some I didn't even understand!). Several executives from the company faced me with my lies in one quick, heated meeting—and I was fired.

I retired the Rome story forever.

I got another job as a receptionist, and he got me fired from that in a matter of two months. At first he only used telephone harassment. When that didn't work with my supervisor, he escalated to dirty tricks. I was sitting there answering phones when four men from the Rescue Squad rushed through the doors looking for the dying receptionist. The Rescue Squad didn't take kindly to false alarms, and it took a lot of fast talking by my supervisor before they were convinced we knew nothing about the false report. I got fired that day.

My next job was with *The Washington Post* newspaper as a copy desk girl in the classified advertising department. This time I anticipated his skip-tracing moves and covered my tracks so that he wouldn't be able to find where I was working.

He changed his tactics and began to follow me in his car as I walked down the street. A couple of times as I was crossing the street, he ran the car through the crosswalk and tried to hit me. I was beginning to believe that he truly meant to kill me. I asked the police for help, but they couldn't do anything unless he actually attacked me. I intuitively felt he was capable of killing me and that I was in danger. (In case you think I'm exaggerating, he has now been put away for life for killing the young husband of a woman he wanted. He shot the fellow five times in front of a room of witnesses.)

The January prior to my husband's release from jail, I had

gone to St. Matthew's Cathedral in Washington and asked to be baptized Catholic. After one session with me, the priest was convinced that I had already had instructions and could be baptized a week later. A co-worker stood up for me as godfather, and later I celebrated what I considered the most important occasion of my life by eating a pint of ice cream in my room. As a new Catholic, the Cathedral became the focal point of my activity, outside of my job. I went to three Masses on Sunday, confession every Friday and the special prayer services throughout the week.

Now, with my fears of being killed, I felt I had no place to turn for help but the Church. I walked to St. Matthew's rectory and requested to see the priest who had baptized me. I was told that he was hearing confessions and that I should come back in two hours. I knew that if I left the rectory, the man following me in the car was going to kill me. So I said it was an emergency and couldn't wait.

When he came in, the priest was furious that I had gotten him out of the confessional. I told him my story. I told it to him straight. No lies. I told him I thought I was going to be killed if I didn't get help. Could he help me find a safe place to stay? The priest listened but I could tell he thought I was a mental case. He told me there was nothing he could do for me. I'd have to get help from the police.

When I left the rectory, I was convinced I would be dead shortly. In an odd way, I was very calm about it. I could feel a heavy cloud enveloping me. But I wasn't frantic. I had resolved that I was about to die.

I was a block from the rectory when I heard my name being called. I looked around and it was the priest calling after me. For some reason, right after I left the rectory he called a friend of his who worked in the police department. She did some quick checking and told him that my story was true and that the authorities in the jail believed this man to be dangerous. She suggested he tell me to go to a nearby YWCA. They were sure I'd be safe there.

From this point on, everything turned around for me and things started "going my way."

My husband simply lost interest in me. I never saw him again until the TV news reports on the murder of the young husband. Even in the newspaper, in the part dealing with his background and history, his marriage to me wasn't mentioned. It was as if I had never touched his life.

At the newspaper, I was working at a job I thoroughly enjoyed. I had been promoted twice in less than a year to a position of considerable responsibility. I was eighteen years old. I was making a good salary. I was learning that I could do good work and hold my own in the adult job market, and I saw myself working at the paper for a long time. With that thought came a sense of stability in my life.

After a brief stay in a girlfriend's apartment, I was able to move into a small, furnished efficiency apartment of my own. I acquired a cat, whom I named Eloise, bought a couple of house plants, even a small TV. I was actually beginning to live like a regular person. The only leftover from the marriage was the divorce procedure—he wasn't fighting that. The Church annulment came through long before the civil divorce because he had been married (legally and in the eyes of the Church) prior to me, thereby making my marriage to a divorced man "null and void."

All my spare time was spent at the Cathedral. I had become friends with the priest whom I had gone to for help, despite our shaky start. He invited me to join a men's lay group called Apostolic Action that had been set up for the purpose of dealing with the multitude of people who presented themselves at the rectory for help. The men in the group had felt they needed a couple of women to work with them.

I was a member of Apostolic Action for almost three years. Each year the twelve of us handled 700 cases. We would go to the rectory every evening in shifts and deal with whoever came to the door: lonely men down on their luck needing a place to sleep for a night or two, people needing jobs, some needing medical care, most wanting money. Several times we worked with the Immigration and Naturalization Service to help get people sent back to their home country—or to keep them from being sent back. We dealt with the basic survival problems—the nuts and bolts of keeping people alive. This freed the priests to deal with the religious and moral dilemmas.

By now, it was the mid-sixties. There was a movement of change and renewal going through the Church. Vatican II was in full operation and issuing changes almost daily regarding structure and tradition. The issue of birth control divided the priests, and, for the first time, I was hearing the clergy express individual opinions about Church policy and position. The morality of the Viet Nam War was being questioned by the younger priests. The idea of war, peace and religion as theological concepts sprang to the fore. The general atmosphere around the Cathedral was one that no longer quietly accepted Church tradition or doctrine. Everything was up for questioning, which suited me perfectly. I was a natural rebel in the Church. I felt it was my responsibility to review every aspect of the Church as it came along and to decide on an individual basis whether or not I could include it in my belief system. I was driving the priests nuts.

In 1966, I made a major decision. One minute the thoughts surrounding this decision had not even entered my mind. The next minute, I had decided I *must* travel to Europe. I didn't know why; I only knew that it was important that I go.

I ripped my office calendar apart and taped each month on the filing cabinets facing my desk, closed my eyes and threw a pencil at the months. It hit the month of January 1967—January 7th, to be precise.

On that day in June 1966, I decided I would leave for Europe on January 7, 1967—for a year. I actually left on January 5th. I had decided to cross the Atlantic by freighter and that was the closest date I could get to January 7th. I farmed Eloise out, gave up my apartment and job, resigned from Apostolic Action, said good-bye to my friends and departed for Europe with a total of $1500 and one suitcase. I was twenty-one.

I left with no itinerary. I wasn't even sure where we were going to dock. Depending on the weather, it would either be Liverpool or Southampton. It ended up being Liverpool. I went to London, then crossed the Channel to Holland. Moved from Holland through Belgium, France, Spain and crossed the Mediterranean to Morocco. Returned to Spain, traveled along the coast into France, Italy, then down to Rome. Arrived in Florence and stayed awhile, then moved on, back to France, into Austria, Switzerland and Liechtenstein, over to Paris, then into Germany and home from Frankfurt.

I hitchhiked from town to town. I visited every Cathedral, art museum and gallery I could find. I knew no languages—except for a smattering of French from my two years at the academy which, for all intents and purposes, was totally useless. Each time I crossed a border, I would learn in the new language "yes," "no," "thank you," "Do you have a small single room?" and "Where's the bathroom?"

I stayed in Florence for three and one-half months to work in the Art Restoration Program that was going on there due to the catastrophic flooding of the Arno in November 1966.

This also gave me time to fall in love with an Italian lawyer who was a Communist, who knew no English and who had a fascist roommate. My little, politically naïve mind was banging and crumbling all over the place. I never thought I would meet an honest-to-god communist, let alone fall in love with one. Weren't these people supposed to have shifty eyes and horns?

Europe showed me that there were many ways to exist, to think, and no one way was better than the next. It broke down many of my embarrassingly naïve preconceptions about my country and the activities of my government. It was a devastating realization for me. I was blasted for our Viet Nam policy in every country I visited. (The Europeans knew what was going on in Viet Nam long before we did.)

I also learned that I naturally gravitated to the simpler lifestyle of the Europeans, to their focus on quality rather than quantity and to their sense of grace and politeness.

I returned to the United States having decided that I would not go back to *The Washington Post*. (Before leaving for Europe, the head of personnel had invited me to rejoin *The Post* after I returned from my trip.) I wanted the essence of the lifestyle I had discovered in Europe, and working with *The Post* again would put me right back into the pressures inherent in large urban newspapers.

Instead, I presented myself at the National Gallery of Art (in Washington, D.C.) and convinced them that because of my

European experiences with major art galleries and museums, and my restoration work in Florence, I would be an asset to them as an employee. They bought that, and I became the first person hired in publications who not only did not have a degree in art history but who had no college education at all.

I found a tiny basement apartment in the home of a young couple on Capitol Hill. Within two weeks after my return, I had re-established myself in the United States.

I also re-established myself with the American Catholic Church. By now, I was even less patient with the things I felt were trivial and meaningless baggage within the Church, and I quickly tired of my local parish church—an ultra-traditional experience, at best. My search for a more responsive, alive Mass brought me to the Newman Center at George Washington University.

At the same time, I began to meet university professors of theology and philosophy. Most of them were priests. Many of them were considered scholars in their fields. They were highly trained men who tended not to want to entertain new thought— only old thought. It was this unlikely group of men who catalyzed my next major shift.

We spent many evenings together discussing minute religious or theological points. In the beginning, I was intimidated by these men and their background—the ol' David and Goliath syndrome. But that didn't last long. I found that what they had to say was absolutely outrageous and I started to argue with them. To simply keep up with the argument, I had to focus intensely on these men and on what they were saying. They excelled at playing elaborate little games with language and thought that were designed to trap lesser adversaries into concession. But there were holes in what they were saying, and I was determined to point them out and not to get trapped. The quality of focus I needed exceeded anything I had previously experienced.

Suddenly, I found myself saying things I had not ever thought about, and I was saying them concisely and clearly. I talked about the quality of man's spirit, the meaning of life on Earth, the relationship between birth and death . . . all of which simply fell out of my mouth. And these men would listen—much to my surprise.

It was also during these sessions that I began to explore the relationship between society and the Church, and the Church's response (or lack of response) to the pressing social issues of the late 1960s and early 1970s. I began to see more clearly the difference between the churchgoer and the Christian, and that the essence of Christianity lay outside the walls of the Church, in the everyday movement of life. This led to my exploration of the concept of nonviolence as a lifestyle. Interest in nonviolence was growing in Washington in those days, particularly in university communities. The white liberals were intrigued with Martin Luther King, Jr., and what he had preached to his marchers. Gandhi became *the* name to drop in conversations. And the liberal wing of the Church was beginning to pick up on the notion of nonviolence, especially as the absurdity of the Viet Nam War became more obvious. I read everything I could find on Gandhi, Tolstoi, Einstein, Schweitzer, Camara . . . anything on nonviolence as a concept, lifestyle or movement.

In January 1971, a newly ordained Paulist priest, a Catholic lawyer and five of us "young folk" from the Newman Center started the Community for Creative Non-Violence (CCNV). All of us, except the lawyer, lived together in a house, thus forming the core of the community. Our intention was to explore and live a nonviolent, Christian lifestyle, become nonviolent activists within the antiwar movement and set up a school that would give classes in various nonviolent concepts. Lofty visions, indeed. It was one of the most violent experiences I ever endured.

I didn't fit into community life easily. (That's an understatement!) At best, the periods of solitude I used for writing were taken as a sign of my being antisocial. But more often, they were taken as evidence that they had a madwoman in residence. I would walk into a room full of people and conversations would stop. Some people would actually leave the room to continue what they were doing elsewhere in the house, others would simply shoot glances my way—I guess they were waiting for me to do something appropriately strange. What I had to share with them that excited or amused me, they simply stared at. Further evidence that I was mad. To add to the situation, my new cat decided she would go into heat every six weeks (instead of every six months) and would take out her frustrations on anyone's leg, lap and especially bearded men's faces. My commune-mates were ambiguous about their feelings toward cats, but this cat was quickly pushing them to the edge.

We also had problems with the day-to-day running of the house. Several of the people had never lived on their own, outside of a dorm situation. One person couldn't cook without dirtying every pot and pan on the block—which drove that day's dishwasher into fits of frenzy and eventual mutiny. Another person couldn't cook at all and took us to the nearby hospital cafeteria every time it was his turn to deal with dinner. One person was a slob. Another couldn't stand the filth.

The only thing that held us together in those first months was our mutual desire to change the world through nonviolence. But eventually things fell apart there as well.

I was thinking about the concept of *ecology* as one facet of nonviolence. In 1971 people were just beginning to talk about ecology. I was getting more and more excited about the concept of ecology as being nonviolence expanded beyond the focus of man to include the environment around him. I wanted to talk about it and stir up interest in a nonviolent, environmental lifestyle. But the thrust of CCNV was moving exclusively toward the antiwar movement. There was no time to deal with something like ecology. Flowers and butterflies and all that frivolous stuff would have to wait. Their rejection of this made me feel even more distant from them.

There were two reasons why it was appropriate for me to become a part of CCNV—neither reason had to do with my becoming one of the "founding fathers" of a nonviolent community. First, it catalyzed my thinking about the concept of ecological nonviolence—man's responsibility within nature, the destruction of nature being the destruction of man himself, the quality of man's existence being directly related to the quality of his link with nature. I quietly tucked this information away in the back of my mind to be used later.

The second reason was Clarence Wright, a Paulist seminarian who lived down the street from CCNV. He worked with the Newman Mass, was one year away from ordination to the priesthood, was interested in nonviolence, and he supported the founding of CCNV.

He was also a young man with the innate ability to heal the torn soul and damaged spirit of just about anyone. After the struggles I was having within CCNV (by this time, I was a member of the walking wounded), I was totally susceptible to his gentle, kind concern for me. And he became intrigued with my strange life and free thinking.

We fell in love like two fools hit by one truck.

His being a seminarian created a slight problem. The fact that he was assigned to work at Newman and lived in the same area as I did, and associated and worked with the same people, made things sticky as we worked to keep our relationship secret for months. In June, he was assigned for the summer to work and study in an alcohol and drug rehabilitation center in Atlanta, Georgia. Our separation became intolerable in a matter of weeks. I flew to Atlanta for a four-day visit over the Fourth of July holiday—and we haven't been apart since.

It "hit the fan" when the Paulists and the people at CCNV found out about our relationship. The priest at CCNV spent three hours trying to convince me that our relationship was nothing more than a figment of my imagination. The head of the Paulists wrote Clarence a letter (when Clarence informed him that he would be leaving) and referred to me throughout the letter as "the problem." Others accused me of snatching Clarence away from the loving arms of the Holy Mother Church. My best friend, the woman I had loved as a sister, refused to talk to me and would have nothing to do with me. Many of the fellow Paulists, whom Clarence considered brothers, shunned him. (I took perverse pleasure some time later when those people who raised the biggest stink about Clarence and me found themselves involved in similar circumstances. Priests left to get married and my ex-best friend fell in love with a priest. . . .) Still, we found a handful of friends—the CCNV lawyer and his family and a couple of fearless Paulists. They were a small but mighty group who supported and helped us to get on our feet when we returned to D.C. in August.

We spent the first ten months working to get financially stabilized. There wasn't a big calling in the Washington job market for an ex-seminarian with a master's degree in philosophy. Clarence managed to land a job tutoring kids in a special education program, but they wanted a lot of dedication in return for a very low salary. I got a job selling human hair wigs door-to-door. Our combined salaries managed to keep us in food and our $135 a month apartment.

My partnership with Clarence also caused me to lose all of my old Church jousting buddies. They could take my somewhat radical thinking on ecclesiastical matters only so far—their tolerance did not include my living with an ex-seminarian. But I soon found myself surrounded by new people—Paulists and ex-clergy who, like ourselves, moved in a more liberal flow within the Church. They were people who were very comfortable with the idea that Catholics should discover and formulate their own theology.

What began to fall out of my mouth now no longer dealt with the broad, generalized scope of reality I had experienced before but rather with more practical questions and functions surrounding the soul—the afterlife, what it meant for souls to be physical, to be on Earth. How did that affect things like our capacity to love? Was being physical confining to our true nature? What was the "nuts and bolts" process of death?

In early January 1972, we got a phone call from one of our Paulist friends. A psychic was going to speak at St. Paul's College that Saturday. He didn't know what she was going to speak about, but he felt we might be interested in hearing her. The psychic was a woman named Peggy Townsend.

Even though she was invited to the college by one of the priests, I wouldn't say she was welcomed with warm, open, loving arms. There were about thirty-five priests and seminarians in a conference room, seated three deep around a long table. Clarence and I were seated at one end of the table facing her.

I had no idea what to expect from this woman. I knew virtually nothing about psychics—only that they did strange things, and I wasn't sure what the strange things were. I also expected a thin, wispy woman dressed in white flowing robes to come floating into the room. She was thin, all right, but she wore a wool pants suit and walked like a normal person.

Many clergy in the room came prepared for her. Armed with their Bibles, they attempted to blast holes in her role as a psychic and in her work by using Scripture. Unfortunately, they picked the wrong person. She happened to be equally versed in the Bible and quoted passages back to them that supported the role of the psychic within Christianity. All the while, I sat quietly across the table from her, watching. She didn't take these men on in a sense of combat. Instead, she did two things: First, she quietly matched their challenges point for point. She dodged nothing. And second, she opened some door in herself, letting out such a wave of love energy that it took the destructive fire out of everyone in the room.

Once the clergy backed down from the Bible battle, she was able to move on to the specific areas of reality that she had been able to explore because of her inner ability. She addressed the areas of death and life after death—just my kind of issues! I started asking her pointed questions based on what I had been learning. Much to my surprise, she verified everything I had been saying. And, for the first time, I realized that all the stuff that had been falling out of my mouth wasn't coming from my fantasy. Here was a woman who was saying exactly the same things—and more.

When the session ended, I said to her, "I think I need to see you privately." She replied simply, "I know," and set a time for the next morning.

I spent the rest of the day quietly in the apartment. My experience with Peggy Townsend had totally disoriented me. All I knew for sure was that I needed to see her. I needed to find out what was happening to me. And I desperately wanted to grab every iota of information she had on the afterlife.

That night, the temperature outside dropped below 0 degrees Fahrenheit. The next morning, we could get only one of our motor scooters started—the smaller one that only carried one person. I had wanted Clarence to be with me when I met with Peggy, but because of the weather I arrived alone.

We went into a small room. I sat in a chair directly opposite her. She asked me to uncross my legs and arms so that the energy could flow through me, and then she explained that she had spent most of the previous night meditating on what she was to say to me. She had felt that there was much to tell me. But every time she considered areas to talk to me about, a steel curtain would drop before her. However, I was not to worry. She was going to try again with me there and see what came up.

She sat quietly with her eyes closed for about a minute, then she began to speak. Little things at first. Clarence had heartburn from the garlic I had put in the spaghetti sauce the previous week and wasn't telling me for fear of hurting my feelings. Other little things about our apartment . . .

She sat quietly again. All the while, I said nothing. She said that the steel curtain had come down once more. So she decided to use another tactic. She asked that it be revealed to her what was to be said to me at that moment. Then she was quiet. I was going crazy. I didn't know what she was doing. All I knew was that I had to keep my legs uncrossed and my mouth shut.

Finally, she spoke. She explained that I had the potential to develop psychically in any area—it was all open to me. But I had to understand a few things first. There would come a time in my psychic growth when my relationship with Clarence would no longer be able to come first in my life. At that time, I should decide carefully if I wanted to continue my development. I could decide at any time to go no further. Also, there were two conditions existing presently in me that were causing the curtain to fall, preventing her from being fully open to me. First was my frantic desire to know, to obtain knowledge about this new world of the unseen. This was blocking me, and it was essential for me to learn to relax, to trust that everything would simply flow to me if only I would relax. Second, there was an awareness, a piece of the puzzle, that was not yet a part of my consciousness, but that would shortly come to me. Without this piece, I could not understand the things she could tell me. But again, I was to relax. Once the piece was in place, much of what Peggy wanted to say would simply fall into place inside me on its own.

The last thing: I was cautioned not to force any of my new awareness onto Clarence. When it came to these matters, he was less open and flexible, and I needed to respect his own sense of timing.

The session ended. It had lasted only twenty minutes. As I got up to leave, we hugged. She wished me her love and support. I could tell she wasn't just handing me shallow, social politeness—she meant it. I walked out of the room, knowing I was about to embark on a brand new adventure.

I wish I could say that I followed the advice I got from her, that it was all a snap, that from the moment I left her, I was relaxed, open and calm, waiting patiently for the cosmos to smack me in the face. But anyone who has ever had this experience of getting information from a psychic would know I was lying. It's one thing to hear this information. It's quite something else to act on what's being said!

Of course, I told Clarence everything that happened with Peggy. She had been right about his heartburn.

Clarence and I agreed that if he ever felt I was ramming something down his throat, he'd tell me to back off. But except for one time, he had always found our discussions about such matters enjoyable, interesting, even thought-provoking. The one time I had pushed was during an argument we had had at four o'clock in the morning when I tried to convince him that there were vampires somewhere in the universe simply because the word "vampire" existed. (For me, the word couldn't exist if the reality didn't exist.) But after being with Peggy, I decided not to ram vampires down his throat!

I didn't understand how my development in the psychic world could ever force my relationship with Clarence to become secondary, and, quite frankly, the thought of it scared me. We both ended up pushing this bit of information into the background, fairly confident that when it became an issue, we'd understand and somehow know what to do.

Not long after seeing Peggy, the mysterious missing puzzle piece dropped into place. Clarence supplied it by discussing a book he was reading about reincarnation.

Reincarnation. That was *the* piece. As soon as he started talking about the concept, I saw a huge, old, arched wooden door open inside of me. Suddenly, a wave of information washed through me. What I had been saying about the afterlife now took on a totally different dimension. A multitude of missing bits of information slipped into the mysterious gaps I myself had recognized existed in what I had been saying. I now saw life—both afterlife and Earth life—from the perspective of the many reflections of the soul rather than of just one reflection.

My new adventure had truly begun.

In the spring of 1972, Clarence and I decided to share the joy of our relationship.

We would invite family, old friends, new friends . . . all to come together for a celebration. The celebration would be centered around a Mass. The theme would be the power of relationships. After the Mass, we would eat and play. The lawyer and his family offered us their home for the gathering.

Everything moved smoothly until we asked a close Paulist friend to say the Mass. He refused. He would not say our Mass unless we made it a wedding Mass and had it registered at the diocese as a marriage.

We refused. As far as we were concerned, we had already created a valid, moral partnership based on no promises, no vows.

I was particularly adamant in this instance. I had grown to believe that it was impossible to promise or vow today what I would do tomorrow. I had accepted Ivan Illich's premise that a vow was not something you took and then hoped to live out. Rather, it was something you earned after many years of living an intent. If we were ever to exchange vows, it would have to be after living together for—oh, maybe fifty years.

Second, if we allowed this celebration to be turned into a Church-recognized wedding, we would be saying that we regarded our personal beliefs as something frivolous, to be disregarded and tossed aside at the slightest whim of the Church. We would also be saying that the partnership we had created in good conscience in August '71 was no longer valid in *our* eyes and that we now wanted the Church to create a valid one for us.

We found another priest to say the Mass. And with seventy-five friends, we celebrated our partnership.

The controversy surrounding our Mass pushed me into my next important spiritual shift. When I first joined the Church, I looked *within* its structure for the essence of Christianity, for what I called the essence of truth. Then, when I focused on the concept of Christianity and its relationship with social issues, and, eventually, on the concept of the nonviolent lifestyle, I saw that the essence of truth was *outside* the Church walls. Now, by standing up to the Church and saying "no" to their demand to have a "proper" wedding, I saw that the true essence of Christianity lay *within myself.* It wasn't in the Church, and it wasn't floating around me. It was inside me.

In January 1973, Clarence went to work for the Xerox Corporation in Springfield, Virginia. His years in the seminary as the in-house electrician finally paid off. Along with the job came a decent raise in salary. We were beginning to live like grown-ups—money, company benefits, profit-sharing. We were even the proud owners of a van—actually, we were in partnership with the bank, just like grown-ups.

We were still living in the same apartment. Well, the apartment was the same, but the rent was now $150. The neighborhood was rapidly being converted into condominiums, and our entire apartment building (all four floors of it) was being taken over by an invasion of roaches seeking refuge from all the disruptive condo construction. We had to think about moving.

When I first moved into Washington in the mid-sixties, I heard about little farms renting for about $35 a month just outside the Washington beltway in the Virginia countryside. The Xerox building was located on the beltway, which meant that Clarence had to drive ten miles from our apartment to work. In a masterful stroke of logic, I figured that we could rent one of these little farms (of course, for $35 a month), and as long as we moved within a ten-mile area outside the beltway, Clarence would still only have ten miles to drive to work. Ten miles in one direction was the same as ten miles in the other direction.

I didn't have to work too hard to convince Clarence that my little scheme was at last worth investigating. The roaches convinced him for me. As luck would have it, the woman I had worked for when I sold the human hair wigs was now in real estate.

One gray, drizzly Saturday in late January, Clarence and I, along with our real estate friend, headed to the Virginia countryside to look for our $35 dream farm.

Ten miles outside the beltway were subdivisions with homes going for an average of $75,000. A rental, we were advised, would be an expensive and unsound financial move. Land on which to build a home, we were advised, would be our most feasible move.

From somewhere deep inside me, I knew we had to live in the woods. That's all I knew. We looked at ten properties that day, most of them in subdivisions with one tree left standing on each parcel of land. Dusk was fast approaching as we got to the tenth property. Actually, we had no intention of seriously considering this piece. It was fifty-five miles from Xerox. But the little real estate blurb said it was a ten-acre wooded lot with two streams. We were driving around anyway. Why not look?

It was nearly dark, it was wet and this lot was half a mile down a rural dirt road. I got out of the car, and as I looked into the woods from the road for about a minute, I was enveloped by an air of absolute knowing. I turned to Clarence and said matter-of-factly, "This is it."

He was stunned.

The first hurdle we had to get over was the fifty-five mile drive to Xerox. On our way back to the city, we timed the trip—one hour and ten minutes. By the time we got back to the apartment and the roaches, Clarence had convinced himself that since he didn't mind driving anyway, he would be able to put up with the commute.

In June 1973, we packed our belongings (including the "Rugged Individualist"), grabbed our two cats and moved to the country.

When we left D.C., most of our friends severed relations with us. Clarence's working for Xerox and our moving to the country, which was akin to moving to Ethiopia, were a signal to them that we had "sold out," that we were no longer interested in caring about human society. To them, that meant staying in the city to fight for the cause of the common man. It did not include working for *them*—the other side, the big corporation. And it definitely didn't include escaping from the reality of life in the city to the idyllic solitude of the country. To give up the fight for decent food in Safeway for the chance to grow our own food in the country was the cowardly way out.

For the first five months we lived in this idyllic solitude, we had no electricity. No lights. No toilets. No refrigeration. No water. No stove.

No problem. We bought kerosene lamps and a Coleman stove. We converted a refrigerator into an icebox by stuffing ten pounds of ice into the freezer every day. Clarence hauled ten gallons of water daily from Xerox, which covered our cooking, bathing and cleaning needs. For the toilet facility, we bought two cinder blocks, a toilet seat and a shovel. We'd go into the woods, dig a hole, put the cinder blocks on either side of the hole, set the toilet seat on top of the cinder blocks and voilà. We thought about building an outhouse, but the electric company man kept saying the lines to our house would "be up shortly." He managed to drag out the word "shortly" to five months.

In October, the electric lines finally reached our house. By that time, we had made two major adjustments. First, we were no longer concerned about the possibility of living out in the middle of nowhere and losing our electricity. Second, we no longer had any rosy, idealistic urges to embrace the pioneer, back-to-the-land lifestyle. For us, a simple lifestyle now included the concept of appropriate technology. A little bit of electricity, at times, can be appropriate.

With our move to the woods came a rapid series of changes for me. I became a vegetarian and immersed myself in the study of nutrition. I also began to relax in a way I had not experienced since my year in Europe. I spent my entire day in the woods, working to clean up the mess made when the house was built. It was a quiet existence for me. There were no houses or neighbors within sight. Rush hour traffic consisted of two cars going down the dirt road at 5:30 in the evening. Maybe a tractor would go by in the afternoon. Clarence was working the second shift at Xerox, which meant he left the house at 2:30 in the afternoon and didn't come home until 2 A.M.—or 4 A.M., if he had to work overtime. Consequently, I spent large blocks of time alone—in the woods during daylight and by the kerosene lamp with a book at night.

I first noticed something different about the woods when I was alone in the house at night. I could feel an energy, and at night it intensified to the point where I would feel uncomfortable about walking in front of a window or by the double glass doors. Especially during the nights of the full moon. It wasn't the fear that I was going to be attacked by something or someone. Rather, it was more a response to being surrounded by intensity—an air of intensity. Nothing hostile.

In 1968, I had read a science fiction book by C.S. Lewis called *Perelandra*. The story centered around the planet Venus (called "Perelandra" in the book), a planet that existed in perfection. Eventually, it was visited by two Earth men—one who embodied good, the other evil. The one could see the perfection in the planet and moved within its harmony. The other was blind to the perfection and moved in destruction.

I felt that our woods, although badly damaged from being logged poorly by the farmer who owned it prior to us, had not lost the spark of perfection and that once the damage was cleared away, the perfection would again shine.

Now Clarence and I were entering the woods. We each possessed the qualities of both men who had gone to Perelandra. As we worked, our goal was to move in harmony, not destruction, but we didn't always know what that meant. Because of the inner struggles we were experiencing in our efforts to discover balance and harmony—the perfection—and avoid destruction, struggles similar to the ones set up in the book, we named our land "Perelandra."

One morning in the spring of '74, I awoke to the sound of voices. Many voices shouted and called at me, but there was no one in the bedroom except Clarence. I saw no group who could account for the shouting.

Frankly, I was scared. Ever since I had left Isadore's house, I had expected that someday I might lose my mind as a result of the pressures I had had to face growing up. But I didn't expect it to happen when things were going so well for me. I said nothing to Clarence about the voices, hoping that I'd never hear them again.

The next morning, the same thing happened. A group of voices calling. Nothing distinguishable. Just calling. They weren't threatening in sound or content. Still I said nothing to Clarence. I needed time to figure out how I was going to tell him that I would have to be institutionalized.

The third morning. Voices again.

I could wait no longer. Obviously, I was disintegrating fast.

Clarence listened to me carefully and then, without missing a beat, he quoted some letter from the New Testament written to the early Christians. Apparently, the early Christians at one point had heard voices and questioned whether or not they were going insane. St. Paul wrote a letter assuring them that the voices they heard were of the Spirit and they were not to be afraid.

Well, I'm not a fan of St. Paul—not after some of his remarks about the role of women. But when Clarence quoted the letter to me, I could feel that it applied to me as well. I couldn't understand the stuff about the voice of the Spirit, but I paid attention to Paul telling these people that they weren't losing their minds.

Clarence showed no apprehension at all about my voices. My declaration of insanity was being rejected, and I was going to have to deal with the voices from another perspective. Clarence suggested that I meditate.

I didn't know what meditation was. The only time I had heard the word was two and a half years earlier, when Peggy Townsend suggested I learn to meditate. I didn't know what she was talking about then either, so I shoved it aside. Now Clarence was suggesting the same thing. He felt that if I meditated, I could find out what the voices were.

That afternoon, I went into the bedroom to meditate—whatever that meant—and I heard a voice. It told me to lie on the floor. I figured I had nothing to lose, so I stretched out on the floor. Then the voice told me to relax my muscles. I followed the instructions the best I could. Then I was told to relax my mind the way I did when I was a child and had wanted to "fantasize."

I shut my eyes and did exactly what I had done as a child. My body felt the familiar sensation of lifting and, at a particular point, it felt as if it had fallen over a lip or off a ledge into space. *That,* I was told, was a form of meditation.

I was then instructed to recreate one of my childhood fantasies. With little effort on my part, I recalled a particular island I used to "go to" and, in a flash, I was once again experiencing that island. *That,* I was told, was a thing called *astral traveling.* All those childhood fantasies had actually been another form of meditation known as astral traveling.

When I pulled myself out of the island and returned back to my original sense of floating in space, the "voice" explained to me that it was important that I spend a portion of each day in meditation, that meditation wasn't just floating in space or astral traveling. It had numerous facets that were open to me if I wished to learn them. All I had to do was say that I wanted to learn, ask for the help and get into the same relaxed state daily. When I thought about the voices I had heard in the bedroom, I was told that I had not been responding to the more subtle urges to move me into meditation and was given something a bit more obvious to deal with.

The "voice" stopped. I waited for it to say something else, but nothing came. I didn't need time to think about whether or not I would pursue this thing called meditation, so I said I wanted to continue and asked for help. There was no reply and I wasn't sure if I had been heard.

The second day, I got into my relaxed state, slipped over the ledge into space—and there was nothing.

The third day, I slipped over the ledge, only this time the space felt different. It was as if I had gone to a higher ledge before slipping over. Instead of empty space, I saw before me forms, like a group of people so out of focus that I could only make out forms. I felt that I was looking at them through a window, and, suddenly, I realized that I had come home—my real home. I didn't know where this place was but I knew, without a doubt, that this was home and that I had left home to come to Earth. A wave of homesickness washed through me. I had a strong desire to stay in this place. Then I realized that even though I didn't consciously know why I had chosen to come to Earth, I could sense I had made a sound decision.

All the forms turned to me, recognized my presence and sent me a collective wave of love that I found to be quite overpowering. At first, I returned my love back to them, but I couldn't keep up the intensity with what they were sending to me. I felt a pressure building in my body—a pressure from the intensity of the "love wave." Eventually, I felt I couldn't take any more, that I would explode, and I began to sob.

It took another half hour for me to release this experience, but I left it having felt my existence not from the vantage point of Earth but from outside Earth, which gave me an entirely different perspective about myself.

The fourth day, I returned to the bedroom, but this time I was nervous. Although the experience of going home was a joyful one, I was frightened by the intensity of it and concerned about my ability to take on such intensity. When I slipped over the ledge, I once again asked for help.

I saw an arched stone bridge over a wide rushing stream. I felt myself walk onto the bridge. I leaned my elbows on the side and watched the water flow by. After awhile, I felt a presence next to me. I turned my attention to my left and there was a young man, about thirty-six, who looked like a Buddhist monk. He didn't say anything, he didn't even look at me. But I felt safe next to him.

Without talking to or looking at me, he began transmitting instructions. It was as if he flowed his mind directly into mine. He started by giving me basics about meditation, and I knew that this was the "person" who was going to help me, to be my teacher.

For the next two years, I met this man on the bridge. Same man. Each day he worked with me.

We spent months on the concept of word energy and how to clear my mind of thoughts. I saw how what I had assumed were subtle, harmless words could so completely create distress in the mind if left there. I learned that it wasn't the word that was the problem, it was the energy behind the word. Each day, I would work on clearing my mind. He had me pull words out of my head, wrap them in brown paper and throw them into the stream. Then I'd watch them float away. I'd go back into my head, find another word, take it out and go through the same routine.

We spent time on the "art" of coming out of meditation. He taught me how to protect myself from outside intrusions such as a phone ringing, how to use energy to cushion my sensation of falling when an outside noise suddenly crashed into my meditative state.

I had the most interesting time during my astral traveling lessons. I learned that while on that level, a person could request that they perform a service to someone in distress. One day I requested to use my meditation time "in service" and immediately found myself on a train in Yugoslavia. Of course, no one could see me. There was an Eastern Orthodox priest on the train. I was to feed into his mind the meditative experience I had had when I "went home." I found him, transferred the energy of the experience from my mind to his, then left. I was told that the priest had been in despair over his life, that the train was going to crash and that he might die. Had he died in that state, he would have had difficulty moving through his death process. When I placed my experience of going home into his mind, *he* experienced it and was able to release himself from despair before death. The next day, I was leafing through the newspaper and saw a tiny filler article in the back pages about a train crash in Yugoslavia the day before that had killed over a hundred people.

I found this type of "work" rewarding and exciting, and for a number of months I requested to be of service every time I went into meditation. Each time was different, and I learned something new about the amazing, unseen complex activity that goes on around us all the time.

Then, I decided to stop. I felt deeply that although this work was certainly valid, it was not *my* true work, and I needed to stop it in order to move on. For me to continue it would be, in effect, avoiding my real work—whatever that was. I haven't done any astral travel work since.

As I moved into this new world, my connection with the Catholic Church became more distant, more nebulous. The Church's attitude in general was not supportive of what I was experiencing, and what I was experiencing had more vital reality than anything the Church could give me. Having found that the essence of truth was within myself meant that I no longer needed the clergy to act as middleman.

On June 12, 1974, I wrote to Pope Paul VI to inform him that I was *resigning* from the Catholic Church as of that date. Of course, we all know the Catholic Church and the Pope could not have cared less about my little letter, but it was important for me to write and formally cut my ties. I had entered the Church—via baptism—with an act of clarity, and I needed to leave with an act of equal clarity.

As soon as I placed my signature on the letter, I flipped into a meditative state which I was not able to get out of for a full twenty-four hours. At first, I saw myself in space, floating, with my oxygen cord connected to a spacecraft. Then the cord was cut and I was free-floating. That was where I remained for twenty-four hours. While floating, I dealt with two strong emotions. One was related to freedom: I was now free to move about in any direction. It was as if the whole universe was suddenly mine. The second involved responsibility. I was struck with the heavy realization that from this point on, my movement, my direction, my very life, depended on no one but me. There was no structure or institution left in my life to fall back on.

In December 1976, I became fascinated with the concept of regressive hypnosis—especially regressive self-hypnosis. I had to learn to do this. I *had* to find out about all those past lives of mine. Since the monk on the bridge wasn't covering this aspect of reality, I was "gonna have to buy me some books" and teach myself.

The next Saturday, Clarence and I went into D.C. to the *Yes! Bookstore* where I found seven books on my newest interest. At one point while we were browsing, Clarence handed me two books and said, "Here, I think you'll be interested in these." I looked at them. Two books on something called Findhorn—*The Magic of Findhorn* and *The Findhorn Garden.* I asked why I would find them interesting and he said, "They're about gardening." I thought, "Oh joy. More books on organic gardening. How boring," and then stuck the books in with my other ones, figuring "what the hell. They're paperback. They're cheap. I'll buy the things and that way I won't hurt his feelings. Maybe I'll get bored this winter and have time to read them."

Now remember my primary purpose for including such an extensive autobiographical section in this book. Everything that happened to me happened for a reason. When Clarence handed me the Findhorn books, that little action didn't come from nowhere. I had gone through years of preparation so that when I got the Findhorn books I was able to read them, understand them and use them as a guidepost to the next significant stage in my life. Everything that happened to me up to that point was in preparation for the next stage. Abilities and disciplines I have now had their roots in my childhood. Hopefully, I've been able to show you those connections.

In a very real way, you are now at precisely the same point as I was when Clarence handed me the Findhorn books. What has happened to you in your life that has led you to the point where you can take in what this book (or any other "instructive" book) has to offer is no less significant to you than my life was to me. Your life may be more subtle or it may be more pleasant emotionally. Or your life may be similar to mine—not so subtle! (I like to call it the "Smack-'Em-Across-the-Head-with-a-Board School of Spirituality.") No matter what, whatever events have brought us to this point are significant—not just emotionally but spiritually as well. It's when we look back and discover the significance of the multitude of events, big or small, that we shift from looking back in misery, anger and fear to gratitude and celebration.

As I mentioned in the Introduction, I offer my life to you as an example (and encouragement) for you to use when looking into your own past. It's very important that you understand the spiritual training you've already gone through—training received from what we like to refer to as the ordinary or the mundane in our lives. You're not just some fool stumbling blindly along. From day one, you have chosen a sequence of events designed to give you a little something to help you along the way. When we recognize the significance of these events, we begin to tap into the wonderful magic we each have in our lives. It's this magic that I wish to share with you.

AN UPDATE OF MY PERSONAL HISTORY

Over the years, a number of people who have read the previous edition of *Behaving* wrote to ask what happened to my parents. How did that part of my story turn out?

Isadore died in 1980. By then, he had been married a total of four times and had five more children. At the time of his death, he was estranged from most of his children. However, he accomplished his first goal in life by becoming wealthy and living a well-appointed life.

Dorothy died in 1988. She had a successful second marriage —with no children. Throughout their time together, she and her husband worked as the crew on a privately owned yacht. She never accepted her alcoholism and continued drinking throughout her life. After she died, I learned from her husband that she had tried several times to stop drinking. But she refused to join AA and, without help, she couldn't stop.

Neither parent re-entered my picture or touched me in a personal way. I kept them at arm's distance by not sharing my life or my work with them. This wasn't difficult for me to do because they never asked anything about my life or what I was doing. For the most part, we remained strangers to one another and we each lived very different lives. Of the two, I saw Isadore more frequently—about once every year or two during the last ten years of his life. Over a twenty-year period, I only saw Dorothy about four or five times. During our last visit, she casually admitted to me that she couldn't stand being around children. I laughed and said, "No kidding!" It was probably the closest moment I ever had with her.

My parents never faced what happened to me as a child. Dorothy needed to maintain a fantasy that our home had been a rich and happy environment for me. I accepted her need for this and didn't challenge her fantasy. We never discussed family history. Conversely, in 1978, I had a strong gut feeling that it was time to tell Isadore what my childhood had been like and what had happened to me after the divorce. After a three-hour session in which I told him the story, event by difficult event, he decided that what I claimed was a lie. He based this on his belief that had his father done to him what I said he (Isadore) had done to me, he would have never spoken to his father again. Since I was speaking to Isadore, it was "proof" that I had fabricated my whole story. When he said this, I looked him in the eye and said, "I'm still speaking to you because I'm a better person than you." It was a triumphant moment for me. Despite his warped logic, I believe that Isadore knew I was telling the truth.

Sometimes people ask me if I have forgiven my parents. I'm always puzzled by this question. I want to ask these people, "Forgive them for what?" I grew up to be a terrific person! I am strong, deeply attached to life and very happy. By age twenty-one I knew beyond all doubt that I could survive whatever life presented me and I knew how to do it. I also knew how to survive my own fears. That's a remarkable thing for a young woman to be able to say. Today when I look in the mirror I see someone I am proud of. These two people played a role in my becoming the kind of woman I am. Of course their role is difficult to look at, even controversial. Had they done to a child today what they did to me, they could have been arrested. However, I was smart. Among other things, I learned from them what *not* to do, and this saved me from making a lot of stupid mistakes. From their sow's-ear parenting I developed into a silk-purse human being. There is simply nothing I need to forgive them for.

After I told Isadore in 1978 what my childhood had been like, he said one thing that showed me he knew I wasn't lying— despite all his other statements to the contrary: "Considering all who were involved, it's a good thing you raised yourself." I agree with him wholeheartedly. It's the smartest and wisest thing he ever said to me.

2

What's This Crap about Fairies?

IMMEDIATELY AFTER RETURNING to Perelandra
that day, I sat down to leaf through my bag of books. No matter
what self-hypnosis book I chose, my attention would automatically shift to the Findhorn books. So I began reading *The Findhorn Garden.*

I could never describe the euphoria I felt as I read this book.
All of a sudden, I was being told that the vague energies I had
felt around me at Perelandra actually had names. Devas. Nature
spirits. They weren't created from my imagination. They actually
existed! What I had felt in the woods was a life force that was
now identified and could be worked with consciously. I saw that
my goal of achieving an ecologically balanced whole at Perelandra lay in my willingness to work with these nature intelligences—these devas and nature spirits. By reading about the

example of the garden that was growing in sand in Findhorn, Scotland, and about how the people who started that garden worked with nature intelligences, I received the encouragement I needed to open to a new world.

One evening in early January 1977, I walked into the woods and announced in a loud, clear voice, "I want to do at Perelandra what they did at Findhorn. I want to work with devas and I want to work with nature spirits. I invite all of you to make yourselves known to me. I am ready to learn from you."

Then I left the woods, returned to the house, put myself into a quiet state and waited.

At the time of my "declaration," I didn't know what I was doing. But years later, I realized that I had used a ceremony to complete a shift that was taking place in me. Ceremony is a physical vehicle used to declare our intent and give definition, direction and purpose to that intent. It's a tool designed to give clarity and form to intent and to make the intent accessible to others. To accomplish this, we use special settings, actions, words, music . . . whatever is appropriate. On that night in January, I moved through a ceremony. I made a clear decision about what I wanted. I chose the woods as my setting. Then I moved through a series of physical actions via the use of words. I stated my intent clearly and simply. Then I sealed my declaration by physically acting on it—by getting quiet and opening myself to whatever was to happen next.

The response was immediate. In fact, I had the same experience that Dorothy Maclean had at Findhorn when she first connected with devas. I had a "crowd of voices" coming at me, all talking at the same time—all telling me that it was "about time."

I connected in with them and found that they had been waiting for this for some time. I remembered that in the Findhorn book, when Dorothy described this experience, she said she simply asked the devas to speak to her one at a time. Having nothing to lose, I tried the same thing. Much to my amazement, they responded instantaneously. And from that point on, I received one devic voice at a time.

Deva (pronounced: day'-vah) is the Sanskrit word for "body of light." I found the devic level to be a level of consciousness very high in vibration. It's as if someone were to hit a bunch of tuning forks and we could distinguish the vibratory difference between them rather than the sound difference. I found the devic vibration to feel extremely high and light. It did not even resemble anything I had experienced in meditation previously. Its essence was clearly different.

The word "architect" has been used by others when describing what devas do—and I, also, find this to be the most appropriate word. For example, it is the devic level that designs the blueprint and draws together all the various energies that make up the complex "package" for the carrot. The Carrot Deva "pulls together" the various energies that determine the size, color, texture, taste, growing season, nutritional needs, shape, flower and seed process of the carrot. In essence, the Carrot Deva is responsible for the carrot's entire physical package. It maintains the vision (the complete reality) of the carrot in perfection and holds that collection of energies together in their unique pattern as it passes from one vibratory level to another on its route to becoming physical to the five senses. Everything about the carrot on a practical level, as well as on the more expanded, universal level, is known by the Carrot Deva.

Each day I would become quietly focused and connect with the devic level. A deva would come into my awareness and identify itself. I was then given instructions. I was told what seeds to buy, what fertilizer to use, how far apart to plant the seeds, when to thin the plants and how much space to leave between them, spacing between the rows, desired amount of sunlight, and so on.

As each deva came into my awareness, I noticed that there was a slight shift in vibration, that each had its own vibration. After awhile, I could recognize which deva was entering my awareness. This led me to develop the ability to call upon specific devas by "aiming" my awareness for the deva's own vibratory pattern. It was as if I was faced with a gigantic telephone system and I had to learn how to make all the different connections. Then I was able to make calls in as well as receive calls.

(Later in the summer, I discovered that all I had to do to connect with a specific deva was to simply request the connection. For example, to connect with the Deva of the Carrot, I only needed to say, "I'd like to be connected with the Deva of the Carrot." Immediately I'd feel the familiar vibration of the Carrot Deva in my awareness. I knew the connection had been made and we were ready to work together. This connection business couldn't have been more simple.)

One day, I felt a very different, more expansive vibration and found myself connected to the Overlighting Deva of the Garden. This deva talked about such things as the overall layout of the garden, its timing, its progression and its shape. From it, I was also told to change my gardening method to the mulch method—a method whereby six inches of hay, grass clippings and leaves are kept on the garden at all times. Two years later, I was told to switch from the traditional straight rows to a garden of concentric circles.

After a somewhat lengthy session with the Overlighting Deva of the Garden, I was contacted by the Soil Deva and given information about soil that dovetailed with what I had received from the Overlighting Deva.

The rhythm of one deva after another contacting me continued throughout that spring and early summer. I wasn't given the "full scoop" on any one subject. Rather, I received just what I was to act on at the moment. Then, at a later time, I got more information. After each session, I jotted down in a notebook what information had been given to me, either practically or as an insight about what I was doing and why. Then, as soon as I could, I acted on anything that needed doing.

To give you an idea of the kind of insight that comes from the devic level, I share with you some examples of the messages. I received this first one on March 22, 1977.

OVERLIGHTING DEVA OF THE GARDEN

We urge you to join our creative process. When you plant a seed, invoke the deva and nature spirits connected with that seed. The seed is the door between you and the various energies that are drawn together on the devic level and cared for by the nature spirits. Once you have planted the seed, put out the call

for the deva to draw together all the individual energy compo-
nents of that variety. Ask that the nature spirits receive the ener-
gies and, in essence, fuse them to the seed. The seed contains the
potential of the plant's perfection. The grounding of the plant's
energy into the seed activates that potential and transforms it
into five-senses reality. As you call the energy into five-senses
form, see its energy channel touch the seed as it is grounded by
the nature spirits.

By joining in our creative process in this manner, you will be-
gin to see the importance of working with the nature energies
with clarity. We urge you to plant the garden in this new way
and see the difference your clear participation as a co-creative
partner with us makes in the germination of the seeds and the
quality of plant growth.

Each of us can receive the same devic message, but because
we are all individuals, we will translate the message differently.
The essence and core of the devic message will remain intact.
Only the precise translation will differ. Because of my personality, I tended to translate all the information I received into action
during these early years. If I couldn't act on it immediately, I
would jot down key words or phrases to remind me what to do
once I began to work with the information. Dorothy Maclean, the
person who received the devic messages for Findhorn, translated
them with great care into words on paper. Because of her concentration and care in this area, she is able to encompass in the
messages the lyrical grace and beauty that always flows with
them. To give you a sense of the difference and a fuller sampling
of what devic messages sound like, I include some of Dorothy's
translation work.

LANDSCAPE ANGEL

I have often told you to think of plants in terms of life, shining life, because this is what they are. Likewise the soil. To us it is a mass of life, each tiny cell or group of cells with a function in the overall plan of life.

The life force in the soil comes through the soil population. It is as though first there was darkness, or inert matter, and then there was light. The light transformed the darkness without which the light could not exist, because darkness, matter, is its mother, its very substance. The transforming of matter or minerals into form capable of a higher vibrational level, what you call evolution, begins at the lowest level and continues up to the highest.

The soil population plays a vital part in this. The natural way a plant pattern comes into form is by using soil, water, heat and air. All these are drawn up into form by the invisible workers in the elements. These you call soil population on one level, fairies on another level. The necessary elements in soil are materialized through fungi; that is why in myths fairies and toadstools are connected.

When humans wish to create with controlled thought, according to how strongly they hold the pattern in their thoughts, the process can be speeded up and the necessary elements materialized almost out of time and space. This is what the cooperation between humans and our kingdom can bring about.

ANGEL OF SOUND

Each plant sounds a note which attracts its builder to it and calls substance to itself through the nature spirits. We devas know the individual notes for all in our charge, and we sound them, like tuning forks, to be picked up by each plant. When a seed is ready to germinate, moisture and warmth do not of themselves set its note vibrating—we do that. We set the seed on its way and hold out its note before it to follow. That note changes with growth and stages, as does man whose voice changes as he advances into maturity.

SPINACH DEVA

As your thoughts create order and unity, as they become more aligned with the whole, so will the forces in the garden become more aligned as well, as what does not fit in will drop out. As you positively hold perfection for each plant in your mind so will it be brought into form.

We are able to work most effectively when we have your creative thought with us, protecting and feeding each plant. It is your garden, you are the creators of it, and we only help as each seed or plant needs it. The overall result depends on your inner strength as put forth in the garden.

LANDSCAPE ANGEL

We see life in terms of the inner force while you see only the outer form and cannot see the continual process taking place. We should like you to try to think in our terms because it will make things easier for both of us—you will be closer to reality and will also be able to understand us better.

These inner forces are as intricate as the outer form, having shape, color, texture, etc., but of a finer and richer substance. When you look at plants, know that what you see has an inner *counterpart simply pulsating with the life you see and much more. As your mind becomes more familiar with this concept and you think of the plants as glowing and moving with life, you will in fact add to that life. By thought, you add to their force and at the same time you draw upon the Source of all life, generating more and more power and more and more life. That is what we all want.*

And finally . . .

LILIUM AURATUM DEVA

We feel it is high time for man to branch out and include in his horizon the different forms of life which are part of his world. He has been forcing his own creations and vibrations on the world without taking into consideration that all living things are part of the whole, just as he is, placed there by divine plan and purpose. Each plant, each mineral has its own contribution to make to the whole, just as each soul has. Man should no longer consider us as lower forms of life with no intelligence and therefore not to be communicated with.

The theory of evolution that puts man at the apex of life on Earth is only correct when viewed from certain angles. It leaves out the fact that God, universal consciousness, is working out the forms of life. For example, according to generally accepted regulations, I am a lowly lily unable to be aware of most things and certainly not able to talk with you. But somehow, somewhere is the intelligence that made us fair and continues to do so, just as somehow, somewhere is the intelligence that produced your intricate physical body.

You are not aware of much of inner intelligence and much of your own body is beyond your control. You are conscious of only a certain part of yourself, and likewise you are conscious of only a certain part of the life around you. But you can tune into the creator within and around you. There are vast ranges of consciousness all stemming from the One, the One who is this consciousness in all of us and whose plan it is that all parts of life become more aware of each other and more united in the great forward movement which is life, all life, becoming greater consciousness.

Consider the lily, consider all that it involves, and let us grow in consciousness, unity and love under the One.

Just about every evening when Clarence got home from work, I would tell him about what I had learned from the devic level that day. From the very beginning, the concept of there being intelligence within nature made sense to him.

One evening as I was chattering on about devas, an arc of light came into my visual awareness. Clarence was sitting across the room in a rocker facing me, and just off to his left was the arc, about four feet high, four inches wide, the shape of a new moon. At first I thought my mind was playing tricks on me. After all, it was late in the evening. I tried to narrow my focus more on Clarence's face in an attempt not to let this "thing" disturb me. But it kept pulsating light at me. Finally, I laughed, admitting defeat to myself, and told Clarence that there was no way I could continue this conversation with this thing pulsating at me. Then I described what I was seeing. He said he had been feeling a presence next to him but couldn't see anything.

Quite frankly, I didn't know what to do with the thing. So I offered it a cup of tea! The thing pulsated even brighter at me. I closed my eyes, first the right, then the left, to see if by chance a piece of lint on my eyeball was causing this strange sight. My eyes were clean. Clarence left the room to make tea—for the two of us, not for our guest—and while he was out, I gave my full attention over to the arc of light. It got brighter still, and, with great gentleness, a sense of awareness washed through me. The light's energy was touching into me. It identified itself as a deva and said it was there to show me that devas were a reality.

This was the moment when the devas and I formally and fully made our connection. When Clarence returned, we continued our discussion with the deva still off to his left. As we talked, the arc of light slowly removed itself from my awareness and was no longer visible.

In February, I was told to go into the woods at midnight to a specific white oak tree. I was to sit by the tree and lean my back against it. There was snow on the ground and a biting wind was making it icy cold, but I bundled up and trudged out to the oak tree. I set a stool next to the trunk, and I leaned my back against the tree.

In less than a minute, I felt a strange energy from the tree flow into my back. My body began to fill, so to keep things from getting "crowded," I decided to use my breath to flow my own energy into the tree. It was a pleasurable sensation—comforting and stabilizing. My body got so warm that when I returned to the tree the next night at midnight as instructed, I didn't bother wearing a coat.

I continued this routine for about two weeks. Then I was told to stop.

During the same period, we were running low on wood for our stove, and Clarence had to find some suitable trees to cut for our supply. I was told by the Deva of the Woods where there stood a dead, perfectly seasoned thirty-foot tree that would be ideal for our needs. I was also told that we would have to enlist the help of the nature spirits in order to get the tree down without doing a lot of damage.

Sure enough, there was the tree, deep in the woods. It was leaning, which meant that the angle of the fall was limited to that one direction. If the tree fell exactly straight, it would do no damage. If it fell no more than two inches to the left or right from this straight line, it would damage a number of healthy trees.

I talked to Clarence about what I was learning concerning the role of the nature spirits. I suggested that when he was ready to fell this tree, he verbally ask for the nature spirits to help in the process. He should state very clearly what he wanted to have happen with the tree and how he wanted it to fall.

Early one morning, Clarence headed for the tree. I was just

waking up when I heard a tremendous shout from him, "No! No! Four feet to the left!" About two seconds later, there was a crash that shook the house. A few seconds after that, I felt myself being kissed gently on the forehead. A clear, precise kiss. No mistaking it for a fly, or the wind. Then I heard a voice tell me that we had "passed the test," the test with the tree, and we were now formally connected with the nature spirits at Perelandra. My energy experience with the oak tree had been my preparation for this moment. The bearer of the kiss was a nature spirit.

Clarence came into the bedroom with a stunned look on his face and explained what had happened with the tree. He asked for the nature spirits' help just as I had suggested, then sawed the tree as carefully as he could so it would fall properly. As it came down through the air, he saw that it was falling way off course— in fact, it was falling four feet off to the right. Because of our conversations about nature, he had become so convinced of the reality of nature spirits that when faced with this crisis his knee-jerk reaction was to shout to them exactly what needed to happen. In mid-air, the thirty-foot tree moved four feet to the left and came down exactly on target.

I refer to nature spirits as "blue-collar workers."

The devas create the package that includes the different components of a plant. Once the "package" of energy is formed, the devas then "hold" the package together as it "travels" from one level to another, changing and adjusting its vibration as it acclimates to the Earth's reality. Once the package begins to take on five-senses form, the nature spirits take over. It is the responsibility of the nature spirits not only to receive the package of energy but to fuse it into its proper form as well. In short, they fuse to a plant its light, its essence, its life pattern and cycles.

Devas are universal in dynamic. My Deva of the Carrot is the same as your Deva of the Carrot. Nature spirits are regional. My nature spirits at Perelandra are not the same as those working around you in your area.

Nature spirits, like devas, can also appear as bodies of light energy. But their vibration feels more dense than the devic vibration does. It is still a very high experience for us to feel. If we could add sound to these different nature spirit vibrations, we would hear clear, high-pitched, pleasing, pure tones—beautiful high notes with soft, distinctive vibratos. By comparison, devic notes would sound even higher in tone, but equally distinctive, pleasing and pure.

Over the years when I've talked about these things with others, many people have said to me that they have had devic experiences—very high, light, pure experiences. As we talked about it more, I realized that they actually experienced nature spirits and thought they were devic because they didn't expect such a high sensation from nature spirits. For some reason, some people think that nature spirits are "lower" in hierarchy than devas. Perhaps even I am fueling this belief by referring to one as "architect" and the other as "blue-collar worker." I don't mean for these tags to imply hierarchy. (Just as when referring to humans they shouldn't imply hierarchy.) They are both equal components of nature intelligence. It's only that they have very different job descriptions.

Nature spirits are the implementors. They are responsible for tending to the well-being of all form and they ensure that the devic rhythms and patterns that create a full life cycle are activated and maintained. To do this, nature spirits "read" the devic information and ensure that this information is fully implemented into action. They also maintain a quality of fusion between the form and the life energies contained within that form. If I were to desire a change in the color of the carrot, I would seek that change on the devic level. That is part of the architectural package of the carrot. However, if I wish to prepare the soil, know the best times for watering the plants and how much to water, I would look to the nature spirit level for help because I'm now focused on the day-to-day issues of the carrot's life cycle.

I had read that at Findhorn there was an area set aside specifically for the use of nature spirits. It was a place where humans didn't enter and it was left wild. I felt that I should do the same at Perelandra. So I picked a spot on the edge of the woods next to the garden and roped it off as a gesture, designating that this area was now to be exclusively for nature spirits. After roping it, I stood in the middle of the area and invited the nature spirits to come to this special place that I called the "Elemental Annex." Immediately, a great rush of energy streamed in and I heard, "Finally! Now we can get down to business!" Feeling very much out of place, I gingerly stepped out of the area. The Elemental Annex was now the base of operations for the Perelandra nature spirits.

Thanks to centuries of tradition, fairy tales and folklore, most people think of nature spirits in terms of elves, gnomes, fairies— the "little people" of the woods. I have experienced nature spirits as swirling spheres of light energy. I have walked through the woods with one of these "balls of energy" moving beside me, and, when necessary, I've moved around a tree while the "ball of energy" continued to move straight through the tree, coming out the other side. My personal inner vision lies in the area of energy. I tend to see waves of energy, energy dynamics and interplay; in fact, I tend to see the reality around me as energy first, then five-senses form. So I'm comfortable with the concept of an energy reality. I was not familiar with or comfortable with the concept of fairies, elves and gnomes. Having read mostly horse books during my childhood, I simply didn't have a background steeped in fairy tales and folklore. So out of consideration for me, when this level of nature intelligence chose to be visible, it chose a context with which I was comfortable—energy. Had I seen an elf or a gnome come toward me, I definitely would have checked myself into a rubber room.

Nature spirits rarely choose to be visible to humans, and when they do, it's for a specific purpose. Among other reasons, it can be to give the person to whom they are appearing tangible proof of their existence, or it can be at a moment of high celebration about something that has been accomplished between the nature

123

spirits and the human involved. I have learned that they cannot be forced to appear at the will or whim of a human. If they appear, it is because *they* find it important to do so.

I have also learned from the nature spirits that they do indeed appear to humans in the form of elves, fairies, gnomes, and so forth, but only to people who are comfortable with these concepts. To do this, they make use of our own thought forms. We humans have developed a long tradition of what, for example, an elf looks like. We have books and stories and artists' conceptions, all detailing the little creatures. Those highly stylized thought forms are released from us and become part of the Earth's reality. When a nature spirit desires to become visible to someone, it has access to this reality and can use these thought forms or combinations of thought forms to aid it in creating a "body" through which to appear. So it is quite possible for someone who has actually seen nature spirits to interpret it as seeing elves.

But there is a reverse side that comes into play here. I've met lots of people who say they've seen nature spirits. When I've talked to them about the interaction that took place between them during those experiences, I've realized that they weren't seeing true nature spirits. The key here is that man cannot *will* a nature spirit to appear to him. But some people want to see them so badly, they actually create their own animated thought form. It's visible. It moves. It talks to them. But it is their own creation and its words are their own thoughts that are being projected through this creation. And most of the time, it makes the person involved feel uncomfortable. And that's the other key. Dynamics of love and balance constantly flow from nature spirits. In my many years of working with this level directly, I've never felt fear or apprehension toward them. I've *always* felt love, balance, protection and care coming from them to me.

We humans have barely begun to understand the power *we* have. We don't realize that out of our own desire, an intense desire, we can create moving thought form. And since these things are our own creation, we give them all their characteristics—even their emotional characteristics. So if we think elves can be mean, we'll create a mean elf. This thought form then becomes frightening to us.

Nature spirits have taken a lot of "bad raps" because of our mistaking our own thought forms for them. They are part of the guardianship of life on Earth. They deal with life forces constantly. They're not in the business of negating life. And it's not part of their makeup to provoke fear in us.

One other thing about nature spirits: they are an extremely powerful level of nature intelligence. They are responsible for the existence of all form around us, and at the blink of a flea's eye, they can remove that form. They are many things, but they are never, *never* cute. Nor are they ever controlled by us. They seek a co-creative partnership with humans, and they are in the position to accept nothing less.

In February, I was given the layout of the garden. Starting at one end, I paced off the rows according to what I was receiving from the devic level. Wherever there was to be a row, I put a stake in the ground, labeling on it what was to be planted there. In previous years, it took me a full day to complete this chore. With help from nature, the process took about a half hour.

Some of the seeds I started in flats in the house—tomatoes, green peppers, broccoli, cabbage, Brussels sprouts and cauli-

flower. I planted each vegetable according to the instructions I was getting. Then I called on the deva and nature spirits connected with the vegetable to ground or fuse its energies into the seed. The response was astounding. Nothing took more than two days to germinate. The tomatoes germinated and had their first set of leaves in less than two days. The seedlings then grew twice as fast as normal. The quality of color in the plants was vibrant. There is a difference in the shade of green between broccoli, cabbage, Brussels sprouts and cauliflower. Now these differences were crystal clear. When I touched the plants, the leaves had a different quality to them. It was almost as if the leaf could barely contain the life that was now embodied in the plant, and to touch the leaf would cause that life to spring from it.

In early March, a full month ahead of my previous years' schedule, I was told to transplant everything but the tomatoes and green peppers into the garden. I was also told to begin the transplanting at 10 P.M. on a specific day. As instructed by nature, I spent the days prior to that getting the plants ready for the big move by hardening them off (taking the flats outside every day so that the plants could get used to the cold and wind).

On the prescribed evening, I took the flats into the garden and began working. The moon was bright, enabling me to see quite well what I was doing.

The nature spirits began to give me instructions on how to plant without causing the plants to go into shock. I was told that the energy of the plant at night was in the root system, making transplanting at night preferable. During the day, the energy was in the stem and leaves. In human terms, at night the plant was in a state similar to sleep. If I worked quietly, carefully and slowly, the transplanting could be done without disrupting that state. This meant the growth rhythm wouldn't be disturbed.

So there I sat on the mulch in the moonlight with my winter coat, hat and gloves on, transplanting in slow motion. I used a kitchen fork to make a hole just large enough for the root ball, being careful not to stir the soil unnecessarily.

As I worked in this state of slow motion, I felt a penetrating air of peace surround me. I felt as if I were experiencing the LeBoyer Nonviolent Birth Method. I was working in gentle moonlight. No noise. All movement was done with great care. And I could actually sense that the plants were not being disturbed.

I worked in this way until 3 A.M., when finally the job was completed. I left the garden in a deep state of peace and inner quiet that I have been able to duplicate only one other time.

Despite the bitter March cold and wind, the little plants continued to grow at a rapid pace. On the nights when we were due to have a heavy freeze, I would ask the nature spirits to protect the young plants, and the next morning I would go outside to find heavy frost everywhere except on those plants in the garden.

As the planting season continued through April and into May, I got devic information on when to plant specific seeds. I then prepared each row with the help of the nature spirits, planted the seeds, asked that the energies be grounded in the seed and welcomed each new energy into the garden.

The first thing I noticed were the different dynamics, different sensations, of each new vegetable energy with which I was connecting. But nothing really surprised me until I connected with the Onion Deva. I had been told that the greatest intensity of energy within the small plants was contained in herbs. That didn't mean much to me until I experienced the Onion Deva that gave me a blast of energy and a force in its communications far more intense than anything I had felt up to that point.

In February, while working with nature to plan the garden, I wondered if it might be good for the garden's overall balance to include carrots. At the time, my garden soil tended toward clay—Virginia is famous for its brilliant red clay. During the previous years, I had worked on the soil and made it acceptable to most vegetables, but I still couldn't get carrots to grow. Actually, it was more like coaxing carrots to drill through brick. But this year, I decided it might be good to include carrot energy and not to worry about harvesting the stubby little roots for food. I asked the Overlighting Deva of the Garden if we should include carrots for the sake of the garden's balance and got a "yes."

Nature was so pleased that I had considered something for the sake of balance rather than food demands that they decided to have a little celebration and show their pleasure. When I asked that the carrot energy be grounded into the seed I had just planted, the nature spirits grounded it all right—in every row in the garden! When I opened my eyes and looked into the garden, there before me were three-inch-high carrot plants sticking up everywhere.

I looked at this for a few minutes and then said, "Joke. Right, fellas?! Just fooling around, heh." (I had heard about nature intelligences and their practical jokes.)

Not really wanting a garden of nothing but carrots, I decided I'd call their bluff. So I stretched my hands out and, with a lot of focus, used my hands to "collect" the carrot energy from all the rows into the one row where the seeds were actually planted. Then I said, "No. No. I meant the energy in this row only, thank you."

Instantaneously, the carrot plants in the one row became six inches high—approximately ten minutes after planting the seed —and the carrot plants in the other rows simply fell over and became part of the mulch.

As part of my effort to have good, workable soil, I put out the call for earthworms. When it came time to prepare the rows for planting, I discovered an enormous amount of earthworms everywhere I cultivated. That was the good news. The bad news was that it was impossible for me to work the soil without chopping earthworms. I wanted them, I got them, and now I was chopping them. Becoming frustrated and angry at the situation, I stopped cultivating, walked out of the garden and announced out loud, "I'm going to have a fifteen-minute tea break. When I return, I want all of the earthworms that are in this row" (I pointed to the row I had been working in) "to be out of the row. You can be on either side of the row, but not in it."

Then I stomped off for tea, fully expecting nothing whatsoever to come of this.

I returned, as promised, in fifteen minutes, picked up my hoe and began working in the same row. The earthworms were gone from the entire row. I was as surprised as anyone could possibly have been—and a little spooked by this turn of events.

I finished working the soil and then thought, if one can "order" earthworms out, one can invite them back in again. So I said, "OK. The coast is clear. I now invite you to come back into the row. I'll give you ten minutes."

I sat down, waited the ten minutes, then went back to the row, picked up several handfuls of soil and found them filled with worms again.

That experience gave me an idea. The moles had taken over our lawn. After seeing what happened to the worms, I sat down on the lawn, got quiet and asked to be connected to the Deva of Moles. I felt a considerable shift but no response. So trusting that the connection was made, I laid out my case about why we wanted the moles out of the lawn area. I explained that I didn't want the moles to leave Perelandra, that I understood they were integral to the life cycle at Perelandra. But would they consider living in the woods or in an open field area about two hundred feet from the house? In either place they could live without being disturbed. Then I suggested that they leave the lawn area at about 9 P.M. Realizing that moles probably couldn't tell time, I changed that to sunset so that they could move to their new areas without being hurt by any of our cats or dogs—who happened to enjoy killing moles. At sunset our animals would be in the house sleeping off dinner.

Still nothing from the Mole Deva.

Assuming my efforts a failure, I returned to the garden. But about a half-hour later, I heard leaves rustling. I looked up and saw a herd of moles—at least a hundred in number—scurrying along the woods' edge, heading for the open field area. Both dogs and all three cats ran toward the commotion, and, seeing that there was absolutely nothing I could do to get the five hysterical animals out of the way, I shouted at the moles, "I thought I told you sunset."

Well, it was like dropping a kid in the middle of a four hundred foot high candy mound. The sight of the hundred moles so overloaded the circuits of our animals that they couldn't move.

They stood frozen in one spot, making noises and scratching themselves out of frustration, while the moles ran right by them en route to the open field.

In mid-May, I discovered that Peter and Eileen Caddy, two of the co-founders of Findhorn, were on tour in the United States and would be speaking in Virginia at the end of the month. I knew I had to see these two people whose books had so altered my life. Clarence took time off from work, and together we went to their one-day workshop.

I received two important bits of information from the Caddys that day. First, they talked about a three-month program the Findhorn Community was giving that winter called the "Essence of Findhorn." As they spoke about it, I knew I had to go to Findhorn and be a part of that program. Second, I asked Peter what one could do if she has already made a connection with nature intelligences and was being run ragged from trying to do everything they wanted. (Since connecting with nature in January, I had made it a point to do everything they suggested as soon as I possibly could. My day was completely at their mercy, and I was exhausted.) Peter gave me a one sentence answer.

"Remember, *you* are the creator of the garden."

All the way home, I kept saying to myself over and over again, "*I* am the creator of this garden . . . I *am* the creator of the garden . . ." By the time I got home, I *believed* I was the creator of the garden.

It was never meant for me to be in the role of the servant. Rather, I was to take a position of equal partnership with the devas and nature spirits. Equal partnership. That meant I had to face my own power and responsibility and not see myself as

someone less than the devas and nature spirits. I was different. Not less.

When I opened this question up to nature, I was told that the relationship they seek with humans is an equal, co-creative partnership. I then saw myself as the conductor of an orchestra who was responsible for pulling together all the individual parts into one harmonious whole. That was my role at Perelandra.

I was also told that I would have to learn to use my power in balance with all that was around me, thus producing the co-creative partnership. I was to learn that if my power became out of balance with the whole, I would then be working in manipulation rather than in co-creation. They told me that one of the main reasons Earth was suffering from its present ecological crises was because of man, out of ignorance and arrogance, wielding his power as manipulator of all around him.

I arrived in the garden the next day with a completely different attitude. I came prepared to assume my position of partner—and I came prepared to learn what that meant. I first announced that I would no longer be available for little projects at three in the morning. I needed a solid eight hours of sleep and time for personal relaxation, so after leaving the garden at sundown, my "office" would be closed. And I would not be available in the morning until after ten.

The response I received was one of gratitude. Both the devic and nature spirit levels are not human, and they needed me to let them know my needs—*my* working conditions. They were eager to adjust their contact with me and take into account my uniqueness. It wasn't that they didn't know me. They were so familiar with the inner me that they geared the information, insights and lessons perfectly to me. But it was important in our partnership that I understood who I was and how I functioned—and to share the information with them. In short, I had to assume my rightful and proper position in this partnership.

By June, I had developed a consistent daily routine. Each morning I sat on a bench beside the garden with my morning tea. First, I "met" with the devic level by connecting with every deva represented in the garden to find what areas, in some cases what plant, needed attention. I used that information to schedule my day. I would then open myself to the nature spirit level, and we would work together accomplishing the different tasks throughout the day.

All the time I was in the garden, I maintained an inner quiet. With each task, I asked the nature spirits involved how best to do the work. As I worked, I would be given insights about what I was doing and why. So my work in the garden was really a classroom.

I came to this garden with a certain amount of foreknowledge based on my previous two years' experience of gardening and on all the reading I had done on gardening and ecology. From this, I formed an inner picture of knowing, called logic. My sense of logic was no longer applicable to the new garden and now functioned as a limitation within me. This limitation had to be broken down so that I could reach a new understanding. To do that, the nature intelligences constantly gave me experiences and lessons specifically designed to break down my sense of logic, my limitation. Consequently, many of the things that happened during this summer of 1977 were startling and often, through the element of surprise, resulted in the crumbling of my frame of reference. What seemed illogical and impossible eventually became totally reasonable—and logical.

My one disappointment was that I would not be sharing in Findhorn's experience of growing a garden under adverse conditions, thus being able to prove to myself (and to anyone else who saw it) that something different was happening here. Findhorn's gardens were growing in sand. Granted, I had the little situation with the clay, but that wasn't nearly as drastic (or impressive) as sand.

But in June, the federal government announced that the entire eastern seaboard of the United States was suffering under severe drought conditions, and several of the states (including Virginia) were declared agricultural disaster areas eligible for government assistance. Even with this announcement, I wasn't overly impressed. I was concerned about the plight of the farmers in the area whose fields were turning brown. But the Perelandra garden was completely mulched, and, according to what I had read about mulch gardening, it was protected from drought. What finally caught my attention was a neighbor who called to tell me her mulch garden had burned out. That's when I knew I was working under adverse conditions, and my new acid test was whether or not I would be able to keep this garden thriving using my connections with the devas and nature spirits.

As the summer months pressed on, the drought worsened. The Perelandra garden continued to grow lush and green. Neighbors (the handful who visited) began to eye me suspiciously.

About this same time, the cabbage, broccoli, cauliflower and Brussels sprouts plants, now quite large, became heavily infested with cabbage worms, a common problem in our area. In the previous years, I had shifted my counterattack from regular, chemical insecticides to organic methods. But this year, I used neither.

A dead bug is a dead bug, whether killed organically or otherwise. I had to consider another solution.

Given such success with the earthworms and moles, I decided I'd connect with the Deva of the Cabbage Worm. I announced that I wished to give one plant at the end of each of the four rows to the cabbage worms. Then I requested that the worms remove themselves from all the other plants, except for the four designated plants.

The next morning, all the plants in the four rows were clean of cabbage worms—except for the one plant at the end of each row. What surprised me most was the amount of cabbage worms on the end plants. Each only had the number of worms it could support—the rest that had been in the row (the sheer number of which would have destroyed the designated plants in no time) simply disappeared.

In less than seven days, the other plants had "healed," leaving no holes in their leaves. As a bonus, the designated cabbage plant formed a perfect four-pound head later in the summer.

As the planting progressed during the spring, the overall energy of the garden changed dramatically. Every time a vegetable was added, I could feel a shift in the energy. The cumulative effect was an energy that felt strong and extraordinarily vital.

In early June, in my capacity as "creator of the garden," I led a ceremony at Perelandra. I declared all of Perelandra a sanctuary for devas and nature spirits, a sanctuary where they could function in partnership with me in peace and together we would work toward full balance—whatever this meant. With that, I invited any devas or nature spirits who wished to join us. As soon as I finished my declaration, many different wildflowers popped up in the woods, and empty flower pots that I had prepared for outdoor annuals were now filled with annuals.

Very soon after this, the intensity of my education was stepped up. I was told by the Overlighting Deva of the Garden that it was important for me, if I wished to continue learning, to gain insight and understanding regarding various dynamics of manifestation. If I were to continue in my position as an equal partner, I needed to understand what was happening around me and the role I, as a human, played in it.

So I continued.

MANIFESTATION: the act, process or an instance of manifesting; to make evident.

MANIFEST: readily perceived by the senses and especially by sight.

I experienced three different dynamics of manifestation.

The first one is a common experience among us all. I need something. I state my need. Lo and behold, a big truck rumbles down the road and just as it passes the property, the very thing I need falls out of the truck. Or somebody walks up to me and says, "I think you should have this," and hands me the needed item. Or, we need a new car and only have $100 to spend. We open the Sunday paper to the "For Sale" section, and there is the perfect car and someone needs to get rid of it quickly—for $100.

I needed hay for mulch. The drought had eliminated everyone's first cutting of hay for the season, and the farmers were holding onto every available bale for the next winter. I was told to state precisely what I needed and to picture it exactly. The devas spent time with me on the concept of clear statement and clear imagery. I was told that although this area of manifestation

138

was the one most readily available to us, we generally botch the process by our lack of clarity. We are beginning to catch on to the idea that we have the power to draw our needs to us. But we have not bothered to discipline ourselves enough to use this insight as a consistent tool—our biggest breakdown being clarity. There is a vast difference between stating, "I need some hay" and "I need one ton of grade B mulch hay."

I didn't know the precise tonnage I would need in order to get through the growing season, so I used other means to achieve clarity. First of all, I was told that when considering manifestation, I was always to contact the deva directly involved with the item requested. In this case, it was the Deva of Hay. (Yes, Martha. There is a Deva of Hay.) I got the insight that I would need hay for two growing seasons—since the drought would cause a hay shortage for the next year as well. Using this information, I asked for enough hay to keep the Perelandra vegetable garden spread six inches deep for two full years.

With that stated, I was told to release myself from the process—meaning I was not to be anxious or worry about whether my request had taken effect. I was to continue my usual daily routine *assuming* that this particular need would be met. I was to relax and, especially, I was not to use logic to learn where the hay would come from, for that would only place limitations on the manifestation process.

Within a couple of days, a neighbor called and gave us the name and telephone number of a local farmer who had a huge pile of damaged hay that he wanted to get rid of.

The hay lasted us exactly two years.

Clarity of thought, word and visualization were the key points emphasized while I explored this first stage of manifestation over and over. When I entered the second stage, I found that I also needed these same three key points.

In July, I moved into an entirely different dynamic of manifestation. By then, I had an intellectual understanding of how nature worked with energy in order to make something physical to our senses. I understood but I didn't *know*—I hadn't *experienced*—yet.

One afternoon, I was told to verbally request and visualize one cubic foot of a specific manure. (It's called starting with basics!) My visualization connected me with the deva of this manure who, in turn, pulled together the various energies for the manure. As part of our co-creative partnership, the deva used the specifications in my visualization to determine the amount of manure to be manifested. Then I was told to connect with the nature spirits and follow their direction.

As soon as I connected, I felt myself lift (vibrationally) to a very familiar level—the level where astral traveling is done. There we waited until, suddenly, I felt a third energy enter my awareness. We had been joined by the energy of the manure. With great care, we all three moved "down" in vibration more slowly than I had ever experienced in meditation—or perhaps it was simply more clearly than I had ever experienced. As we moved from one level to the next, I could feel the shift in the manure energy. Eventually, I felt the manure take on a sense of physicalness—I sensed atoms, then molecules, then cells. I sensed form within the nature energy—and eventually, even a slight smell. When I felt it had completed its process, I opened my eyes, and there before me was the cubic foot of manure.

I'm not going to say that I took this casually. For some time, I just stared at the manure, thinking about what had happened.

141

Then I touched it. It was perfectly rotted, finely textured manure —with not much odor, a testament to its well-rotted state. I poked at the pile until I was totally convinced that there was indeed a pile of manure sitting on the ground in front of me. I asked what I was to do with the manure and was told by nature to spread it on the garden where it was needed. (Of course. How silly of me.)

This manifestation process took about two hours. It had been "slowed" for my benefit so that I could experience the various sensations. Subsequently, whenever I was invited to join in manifestation, it always took as long as I needed to experience and learn new things about the process, and never was it the same amount of time. Manifestation in its "natural state," shall we say, occurs within the proverbial twinkling of an eye.

After a week's experience, I was given a variation of this manifestation. This time as the item we were to manifest took on atomic structure, the nature spirits released from the process and let me aid it alone through the final stages into five-senses form. We agreed, on the devic level, to materialize a squash seed, which I then visualized, once again setting off the process. Then, with the nature spirits, I moved to the appropriate level, felt the connection with the seed energy, moved down with the process and, as the seed became atomic, I felt the nature spirits release from my awareness. My initial impulse, which turned out to be correct, was to use my inner focus to "hold" the individual energies together. I could feel that on the atomic level the energies began to mesh together, attracting more to themselves, thus giving the sensation that the package of individual energies was becoming a physical whole. As we moved through the process, that sensation became stronger. I also found that in order for me to properly "hold" the energies together, it was important that my own vibration match their level. In essence, I couldn't assist the energies on the atomic level if my own vibration was geared to the level where I could astral travel.

At the very end of the process, just as the seed was about to become physical, I had to sharply intensify my inner focus on the seed energy and once again visualize the actual seed in its physical form. That's when I felt the final sensation of form taking hold within the energy. I opened my eyes and directly before me was the seed.

I was invited to continue working in this particular stage for a couple of weeks. Each day an agreement would be reached between the devic level and myself about a particular need in the garden or around Perelandra—seeds, fertilizers, plants, tools . . . anything. And then we'd go to work. The quality of focus—the intensity of focus—required from me during the process was far greater than I ever had experienced. Sometimes I got sloppy with my focus and everything came to a halt. Sometimes I lost the focus altogether, and the energy package would release, move back to the devic level and disperse into its individual components once again. Sometimes if I wasn't able to pull together the exact amount of intensity needed just prior to the thing becoming physical, I would open my eyes only to find it sitting twenty-five feet or so away from me.

Tools were an interesting lesson. First I had to get over my prejudice against tools actually being under the domain of nature. But I found that each tool had a deva, a consciousness. Also, with tools I experienced the demanifestation process—a reverse action that removed the tool from its physicalness and returned it to its energy state.

By the end of July, I was feeling fairly confident about what I was doing. Of course, I wasn't allowed to remain in that state for very long. There was a third stage of manifestation yet to come.

This time I was told to open to the devic level. From that level I was "raised" to another level, one that was also very familiar to me. This time I found myself in the Void—a space I had experienced when I was receiving my early lessons from the monk. (After ending my astral traveling lessons and experiences, I had spent the next six months experiencing the Void.) I was brought out of the Void to the level just "below" it. If the Void is the space where nothing can be distinguished from anything else, not even from myself, yet all that exists is present, then the space just below it is where individuality *first* takes on its characteristics.

I was told that all the individual energy components that are called together by the deva to form a package come from what I call the Void. In essence, all that is, is created from Oneness. I was also told that on the level just below the Void, I could shift my awareness (through intent) and experience, actually *become,* anything else. For example, I could shift my consciousness and become a hammer.

This is very difficult to describe in words. It's hard for us to believe that we can actually release from the awareness of our own existence, our own individuality, and become something else. But on the level just outside the Void, where individuality is at its point of least delineation, this is quite simple.

With these insights, my experience with the manifestation process changed. Once there was agreement on what to manifest, I would then shift to that space just below the Void and will myself to become what was to be manifested, to share in its consciousness. After coming out of that level, I could reflect on what I had learned from the experience, and after considering how I planned to use the item, I could make the decision as to whether or not this particular item would suit the purpose perfectly. Remember, in my role as "creator of the garden" and co-creative partner, whatever I visualized was manifested. Sometimes I made dumb decisions. We'd go through the whole process, and, at the end, I'd find that my original decision had been faulty and what I now had before me was not perfectly suited for the job. This is when demanifestation came in handy. However, by first becoming the thing, I was able to know beforehand if my decision was correct.

Once I activated the process (after having become the thing and making the decision as to its appropriateness), I opened to the devic level and experienced the various energies being drawn together. I then moved through the levels with the deva, felt the shift to the nature spirits, continued through the process and, at the atomic level, took responsibility for the energy myself until it was form and visible.

My experience with manifestation is not something I take lightly. It is a complex, deep, intense . . . quiet . . . experience on every level. I never materialized anything without first being invited to participate. I also got an agreement from the devic level on the precise item to be made physical. From the beginning, I knew that I wasn't experiencing this process in order to use it as a tool to "get rich quick" by manifesting indiscriminately. Nor was it meant for me to use as a parlor trick to razzle-dazzle friends. I'm frequently the recipient of every psychological pressure imaginable, designed to get me to do "just one trick." But

I've learned there are three categories of people. One is the group that will hear what I have to say about manifestation, and it will simply hit the right chords and they'll know that manifestation as I have described it is part of reality. The second group are the fence-sitters. They won't make a decision one way or the other unless they see just one more piece of evidence . . . and one more piece . . . and one more piece. . . . The third group are the confirmed skeptics. They are particularly adept at trying to pressure me. If I do it just one time for them, they'll believe, etc., etc.

If I manifested an elephant, the first group would consider my action unnecessary, even frivolous. The second group would say, "That's fine. But let's see you manifest a sherman tank." The third group, after goading me into action, would then accuse me of dabbling in Las Vegas magic and brand me a charlatan. I'd end up with a confused elephant and three groups of dissatisfied people glaring at me.

I didn't experience manifestation for this. In order for me to continue my work with nature on a deeper level, I had to know, down to my very core, what it meant for something to become physical to our five senses—that the principle of creation is not just reserved for humans. It is a process shared by *everything*. If I were to achieve my goal of moving through life as a participant in ecological balance and wholistic harmony, I'd have to learn to respect the God in all life, all things around me. This meant I had to experience the God in all life on many levels—including the levels of creation and manifestation.

Several people have suggested that I not share with others my experiences with manifestation. They fear that someone will take my information and use their power to force something to materialize. In essence, they might use their power to manipulate. Manipulation is exactly the thing we need to get away from. It's the thing nature has to deal with constantly when dealing with humans. We know very well how to use our power to manipulate the reality around us to conform to our personal whims. But I felt that the person interested in manipulation already has access to information far more detailed than what I have here—the volumes of material written on black magic. There's very little written about manifestation as a natural, balanced, cooperative, co-creative process. We shy away from the concept of black magic, as well we should. But we can no longer shy away from the universal laws of manifestation. We need to understand this aspect of our reality if we are to become equal partners with all on Earth.

My summer was not yet over.

Just as our corn crop began to tassel, it was attacked—ravaged is more to the point—by Japanese beetles. They ate the pollen and demolished the silk. Now, the normal process with corn is that the pollen falls from the tassel onto the silk, thus pollinating the silk. It's the pollination of the silk that causes each kernel of the ear to fill out. Without pollen and silk, one ends up with an ear of corn with no kernels. This summer, if I wanted to salvage any corn, I had to deal with the Japanese beetle.

Based on my continuing luck with the moles, earthworms and cabbage worms, I decided I would contact the Deva of the Japanese Beetle. Much to my astonishment, I touched into an energy that I can only describe as that of a battered child. It was an energy of defeat, of being beaten into submission. Yet it still had mixed in with it anger and a strong desire to fight for its life.

I was told by the deva that what I was experiencing was not devic but from the consciousness of the Japanese beetle itself. I needed this experience in order to understand what our relationship with the beetle had already done to it before I made any requests on the devic level about removing it. You see, the Japanese beetle is not indigenous to the United States. It was introduced to our country by one person who brought in several beetles to be part of his insect collection but accidentally released them. They do not have enough natural predators here, and they have multiplied into a serious problem for our agricultural industry. Consequently, for the past fifty years or so, we have waged a war against the beetle. What I touched into was the result of that war.

Under the circumstances, I felt I had no right to ask anything of the beetle. So I simply asked that the beetle recognize Perelandra as a sanctuary and invited it to join us so that it could begin to heal. I stated that we would not damage or destroy the beetles and would make every effort to enhance its healing process. To seal the bargain, so to speak, I stated that we would leave unmowed a specific area of tall grass that was a favorite of the beetle.

I then addressed the issue of the corn. Still hoping to salvage some of it, I decided I would try to raise the vibration of the individual stalks—perhaps the ears would fill out in spite of the Japanese beetle. I spent three days putting my hands on each stalk and LOVING it. At the end of three days, nature had had enough of this nonsense and I was told to leave the corn patch and not return "until further notified."

Devas and nature spirits do not respond to what they call

148

"gooey, sentimental love." Their love is a love of action and purpose, and it is that kind of active love they desire from us. (Once
while giving a workshop, I was asked to accompany several of
the leaders of this particular community to a bush. It was a rather
large bush, and it didn't take a horticulturist to see that it was
dying. It seems they had recently transplanted the bush, and, as
part of their transplanting process, several members in the community would form a circle around it each evening, join hands
and send the bush love . . . *LOVE*. The bush had the nerve to
start to die on them anyway. I was asked what they should do. I
walked up to the bush, looked at the soil around it, checked the
leaves, then turned around and said, "Try watering it." That's
love in action. Not to be confused with loveless action. Love in
action is appropriate action done in a caring spirit.)

I stayed away from the corn patch for three weeks, until one
morning I was told to return. I found that every ear of corn had
filled out—but not fully. Only half filled out. The devic pattern
of the corn had shifted, making it possible for the ears to mature
without using the natural tassel/pollinated silk process. I was told
that half the ear had matured because *this* planting of corn was to
be fed to the birds at Perelandra for the winter, and only the
amount that was needed matured. A later planting standing right
next to this corn, and not yet damaged by the beetle, would be
for our use exclusively and would be allowed to fully mature in
the natural process.

A month later, the second planting matured untouched.

In the years since making the agreement with the Japanese
beetle, I notice that they have increasingly become more calm
and fewer in number. For several years, they damaged only the

roses. Still, I didn't disturb them. It wasn't easy, since my natural impulse was to whack them off the rose bushes. But after some mental adjustments on my part, I could actually invite them to enjoy the roses. Now they do not "flock" to the roses, but I'll still see a manageable number on the bushes from time to time. Because of the shifts and changes on the part of the beetles *and* the gardener, I've found that I have not had reason to request anything special from them. Their presence here feels in balance.

Starting in mid-August that summer, my days became quite difficult to manage. I received word from Findhorn that I had been accepted into the Essence of Findhorn program. I was to report to Findhorn the first week of November. That gave me a little over two months to get the food in for the winter, prepare for my trip to Scotland and close down the garden.

With these pressures, I changed my attitude toward the way I approached the garden. I no longer had time for leisurely morning teas, and I certainly didn't have time to do everything in the garden that was being suggested. So I tended to enter my morning devic meetings much like a drill sergeant. "OK. What needs to be done?" (Listen.) "Fine. I'll do this, this and this, but the other stuff will have to wait."

Soon after this, I arrived one morning to find that the row of Brussels sprouts plants—that had grown to stand a perfect three feet tall—had been attacked by a horde of bugs, leaving the leaves badly damaged and the plants weak.

I couldn't believe what I was seeing. I connected with the Deva of the Brussels Sprout to find out what was going on. I was told:

When you look at the garden now, you see a half-empty glass. You focus on the negative. You deal in only the work to be done.

You no longer see the beauty and what is being accomplished here. Your attitude has unbalanced the energy of the garden, leaving it vulnerable to being overpowered and destroyed by insects. Since you have altered the balance, it is important for you to re-establish the balance. You must understand the power contained in thoughts and attitudes and the integral part they play in the balance of the whole.

I needed to return to the garden, but more importantly, I needed to recapture the attitude that I had had throughout the summer. It wasn't easy. I found it quite difficult to drop all else and refocus exclusively on the garden.

It took me three days to rebalance the garden. Mostly, I concentrated on seeing the garden in terms of its accomplishments and beauty. At the end of the three days, the bugs had vanished from the Brussels sprouts plants, and the plants had started a healing process.

Now the key to maintaining the garden's balance was attitude. It wasn't the amount of work that had thrown the energy off, it was the attitude with which I was working: Pressed. Concerned. Worried. Anxious about the trip. When I finally left to spend more time with my other responsibilities, I made it a point to move in and out of the garden in a clear, settled, quiet state of mind. With this, the garden balance held.

I felt from nature that it was important to wait until after the first heavy frost and not rush the job of "putting the garden to bed," preparing the garden for winter. I waited and waited for that frost, and for awhile it looked as if I would have to set off for Findhorn, leaving the job for Clarence.

Finally the frost hit. I moved into the garden to do the last process, thus completing the season's cycle.

What I had assumed would take one day actually took seven full days. It was a most extraordinary experience, very similar to the nonviolent birth experience. Only this time, it was nonviolent death. I spent seven days touching into each energy that had become part of the garden. I thanked it for its presence, then released it from the garden. I found that even if the form of the plant was dead, the energy, the consciousness of the plant, had remained a part of the whole energy of the garden. As I released it—either by removing the plant or touching into the energy and simply requesting that it release—I felt it leave my own awareness. The nature spirits that had worked with that vegetable left the garden and faded into the Elemental Annex. Everything had to be done gently and slowly, respecting the fact that this growing cycle was over, and we were going into a period of rest and peace. The atmosphere around me was calm—very calm. Every move I made was slow but deliberate and precise—it was clarity in motion. All the time, I stayed in contact with the specific consciousness with which I was working.

It's difficult to communicate this experience because of its depth, its extraordinary mixture of peace, gentleness and love, and because it was happening on different levels simultaneously, both inside me and outside me. In retrospect . . . it had to be the deepest time.

3

The Lessons Continue

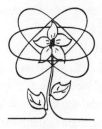

I RETURNED FROM FINDHORN in March '78 in a
deep state of "shell shock." Once the community members at
Findhorn believed I wasn't some weird, half-crazed broad who
had just fallen out of some tree and that my experiences in the
garden were, in fact, real, they asked me to talk. And talk and
talk and talk . . . At first, I was flattered by the interest and attention. And my talking about the garden enabled me to feel less cut
off from Perelandra.

But during the last week there, I began to question whether or
not I had talked *too* much. In my enthusiasm to share everything
as completely as I possibly could, had I broken some covenant,
some trust, between myself and nature? Was it possible that what
had happened between us was meant to be secret? I was new to
this remarkable world of nature intelligence and ignorant of the

correct protocol. I wasn't even sure there was a protocol of which to be ignorant.

When I left Findhorn, I braced myself for the possibility that my education in the garden was over. Of course, I was wrong. Working with nature did not make me a member of some secret society. I didn't understand the extent of how wrong I was until I started working in the garden again. From our first meeting, I could tell that I had lost nothing in my co-creative partnership and, in a short time, I was full-speed into a new year, a new garden, new lessons.

REALITY AS ENERGY — ENERGY AS FORM — FORM AS NATURE

The one theme that ran throughout all my lessons this second year was energy. Not the stuff you can put in cars. Not fire. But energy: the reality behind five-senses form. It's the first key to shifting our awareness and understanding about nature. The second key is to understand that inherent in all energy is intelligent consciousness. In fact, intelligence is one of the dynamics that makes up energy.

When I was at Findhorn, I led a meditation given to me by nature that was designed to bring people in touch with the intelligent consciousness contained within all matter. Each person chose an object—then I led them through the meditation. I had never led a meditation, so I fully expected nothing to happen. I even told the people not to worry about it if the whole thing flopped. When we finished, everyone sat very quietly. I asked them to share what had happened, if anything at all. One by one, they shared. Nearly everyone in the room had been in communication with their object. We were all rather stunned—they, for having actually gone through the experience of being in communication with a "thing," I for the obvious ease with which this meditation succeeded.*

Later that day, I reconnected with nature and asked why the meditation had worked so well.

Man can no longer afford to look at what exists outside himself as nothing more than five-senses form—in most cases, lifeless form. He must also begin to see the reality around him in terms of energy. And with this, he must understand that contained within all energy is intelligent consciousness—life. This meditation is but one tool designed to aid humans in expanding their awareness. The time is now and the shift is crucial. Those sensitive to and at ease with the timing will shift their awareness with relative ease through the aid of such tools as this meditation.

As the years roll on and my lessons with nature continue, I see that there is a third key to shifting our awareness and understanding about nature. This has to do with how we define nature itself. Usually, when we think of nature, we think of rocks, rivers, mountains, clouds, birds, deer, trees, flowers. . . . But nature is actually much more than this.

In 1990, I asked nature to define itself. In order to understand the definition, they said I had to first allow nature to define form.

---

* You may experience the Object Meditation for yourself. We offer it on tape. See the Afterword for how to receive our catalog.

FORM: *We consider reality to be in the form state when there is order, organization and life vitality* [initiates action] *combined with a state of consciousness. . . . We do not consider form to be only that which can be perceived by the five senses. In fact, we see form from this perspective to be most limited, both in its life reality and in its ability to function. We see form from the perspective of the five senses to be useful only for the most basic and fundamental level of identification. From this perspective, there is very little relationship to the full under- standing and knowledge of how a unit or form system functions.*

All energy contains order, organization and life vitality; there- fore, all energy is form. If one were to use the term "form" to identify that which can be perceived by the five senses and the word "energy" to refer to that aspect of an animal, human, plant or object's reality that cannot be readily perceived by the five senses, then one would be accurate in the use of these two words. However, if one were to use the word "form" to refer to that which can be perceived by the five senses and assume that form to be a complete unit of reality unto itself, and use the word "energy" to refer to a level beyond form, one would then be using these words inaccurately. From our perspective, form and energy create one unit of reality and are differentiated from one another solely by the individual's ability to perceive them with his or her sensory system. In short, the differentiation be- tween form and energy within any given object, plant, animal or human lies with the observer.

On the planet Earth, the personality, character, emotional makeup, intellectual capacity, strong points and gifts of a human are all form. They are that which gives order, organization and life vitality to consciousness.

Order and organization are the physical structures that create a framework for form. In short, they define the walls. But we have included the dynamic of life vitality when we refer to form because one of the elements of form is action, and it is life vitality that initiates and creates action.

NATURE: *In the larger universe and beyond, on its many levels and dimensions, there are a number of groups of consciousness that, although equal in importance, are quite different in expression and function. Together, they make up the full expression of the larger, total life picture. No one piece, no one expression, can be missing or the larger life picture on all its levels and dimensions will cease to exist. One such consciousness has been universally termed "nature." Because of what we are saying about the larger picture not existing without all of its parts, you may assume that nature as both a reality and a consciousness exists on all dimensions and all levels. It cannot be excluded.*

*Each group of consciousness has an area of expertise. As we said, all groups are equal in importance but express and function differently from one another. These different expressions and functions are vital to the overall balance of reality. A truly symbiotic relationship exists among the groups and is based on balance—universal balance. The human soul-oriented dynamic is **evolution** in scope and function. Nature is a massive, intelligent consciousness group that expresses and functions within the many areas of **involution**, that is, moving soul-oriented consciousness into any dimension or level of form.*

Nature is the conscious reality that supplies order, organization and life vitality for this shift. Nature is the consciousness that is, for your working understanding, intimately linked with form. Nature is the consciousness that comprises all form on all levels and dimensions. It is form's order, organization and life vitality. Nature is first and foremost a consciousness of equal importance with all other groups of consciousness in the largest scheme of reality. It expresses and functions uniquely in that it comprises all form on all levels and dimensions and is responsible for and creates all of form's order, organization and life vitality.

Take a minute to think about this. Nature is saying that it is the order, organization and life vitality of all form and that all form contains consciousness. The first important point nature is making is that all form—that is, anything that has order, organization and life vitality—is nature. This goes way beyond the common notion that nature is trees, birds and rivers. This book is form. Its pages and ink are form. They have order, organization, and the molecules have life vitality. Therefore, this book, its pages and ink are all nature because nature supplies all order, organization and life vitality. The chair you are currently sitting in (assuming you are sitting) is nature. The walls surrounding you are nature. Everything in the room you are sitting in is nature.

To expand this point: Remember that chart from high school chemistry class? The "chart from hell." The chart we swore we would never look at again if only we could escape from that class in one piece. Well, it's back. Look at it carefully. (There will be a test.)

PERIODIC TABLE OF ELEMENTS

period	Ia	IIa	IIIb	IVb	Vb	VIb	VIIb	VIII			Ib	IIb	IIIa	IVa	Va	VIa	VIIa	o
group																		
1	1 H hydrogen																1 H hydrogen	2 He helium
2	3 Li lithium	4 Be beryllium											5 B boron	6 C carbon	7 N nitrogen	8 O oxygen	9 F fluorine	10 Ne neon
3	11 Na sodium	12 Mg magnesium											13 Al aluminum	14 Si silicon	15 P phosphorus	16 S sulfur	17 Cl chlorine	18 Ar argon
4	19 K potassium	20 Ca calcium	21 Sc scandium	22 Ti titanium	23 V vanadium	24 Cr chromium	25 Mn manganese	26 Fe iron	27 Co cobalt	28 Ni nickel	29 Cu copper	30 Zn zinc	31 Ga gallium	32 Ge germanium	33 As arsenic	34 Se selenium	35 Br bromine	36 Kr krypton
5	37 Rb rubidium	38 Sr strontium	39 Y yttrium	40 Zr zirconium	41 Nb niobium	42 Mo molybdenum	43 Tc technetium	44 Ru ruthenium	45 Rh rhodium	46 Pd palladium	47 Ag silver	48 Cd cadmium	49 In indium	50 Sn tin	51 Sb antimony	52 Te tellurium	53 I iodine	54 Xe xenon
6	55 Cs cesium	56 Ba barium	57 La* lanthanum	72 Hr hafnium	73 Ta tantalum	74 W tungsten	75 Re rhenium	76 Os osmium	77 Ir iridium	78 Pt platinum	79 Au gold	80 Hg mercury	81 Tl thallium	82 Pb lead	83 Bi bismuth	84 Po polonium	85 At astatine	86 Rn radon
7	87 Fr francium	88 Ra radium	89 Ac** actinium	104 Rf *rutherfordium*	105 Ha *hahnium*													

* 6	58 Ce cerium	59 Pr praseodymium	60 Nd neodymium	61 Pm promethium	62 Sm samarium	63 Eu europium	64 Gd gadolinium	65 Tb terbium	66 Dy dysprosium	67 Ho holmium	68 Er erbium	69 Tm thulium	70 Yb ytterbium	71 Lu lutetium
** 7	90 Th thorium	91 Pa protactinium	92 U uranium	93 Np neptunium	94 Pu plutonium	95 Am americium	96 Cm curium	97 Bk berkelium	98 Cf californium	99 Es einsteinium	100 Fm fermium	101 Md mendelevium	102 No nobelium	103 Lr lawrencium

Every element listed in this chart is found within nature. They are the fundamental materials of which all matter is composed. Every element on this chart—every molecule—has its own order, organization and life vitality. By combining them, we get vinyl, nylon, polyester—and even plastic. The materials for these products are all found in nature and are listed on the Periodic Table. It's just that they are combined in a way that produces what we call vinyl, nylon, polyester and plastic.

For example: We would all probably agree that Dacron is not a natural fiber. It is a synthetic polyester fiber, and we don't harvest polyester fibers from the field. The following is the chemical makeup of Dacron:

$$\underline{heat}\ (OCH_2CH_2 - O - CO - \boxed{O} - CO -)Y\ +\ (Y\text{-}1)H_2O$$
$$(C_6H_6)$$

Dacron is nothing more than carbon (C), hydrogen (H) and oxygen (O), all elements found in nature, that have been specially combined in a lab by a process called polymerization. (Don't let this word scare you. Polymerization is a scientific term for the chemical process used to make grossly fat molecules.)

Generally, when I bring up plastic and Dacron with others, a debate breaks out. Just because the elements exist and can be combined in this way, should we combine them? Isn't this manipulation of nature at its worst? And look at the mess these kinds of products have caused our ecology. I weigh into the debate with this: Imagine a chemist in his laboratory working in a co-creative partnership with nature. The products that would come out of this lab would all be environmentally sound. In such a co-creative partnership, nature would not consider a development that was out of balance with its immediate environment and the larger planetary environment. To operate in such an imbalanced manner would "go against" everything that nature is and how it functions. So the chemist working in a co-creative partnership with nature would be directed to develop products that would address the issue at hand *and* be environmentally responsive. This is what a co-creative partnership with nature can give us.

A major block with how we perceive what constitutes nature is what we think when we use the terms "natural" and "unnatural." Generally, we consider something to be natural if it is a material or element that is found growing or existing on the planet that is then modified and used by humans. For example, raw cotton is harvested from the field, made into fiber threads that then become cloth. This eventually becomes a shirt. We consider an all-cotton shirt natural—yet you can't go out into a field and harvest a shirt. We consider something to be unnatural when two or more natural elements are combined by man to create a third element that bears little or no resemblance to its original elements. Examples are cement, chemical fertilizers, plastics and (get ready for another mind bender) . . .

A garden. A garden is not natural. It is man-made. You don't go out in the wild and run across a free-growing vegetable garden containing beans, broccoli, tomatoes, eggplant and okra. We invented gardens. We got tired of all that hunting and foraging and decided to centralize our food supply. So we collected seed from various plants growing in the wild and planted the seed in one, easy-to-access location. Thus, we created something that did not previously exist.

I read that someone said a garden is man's attempt to conquer nature. Whoever said this had a point. Generally, plants in the wild automatically grow where conditions are conducive to their growth. When they are centralized in a garden location, they are removed from their supportive environment and placed in an "unnatural" environment. This creates massive imbalance. Traditional and organic gardeners attempt to "conquer" the situation by restoring a balance that accommodates their definition of a garden and how it is to function. Co-creative gardeners work in a conscious partnership with nature to create an environmentally balanced biosphere on all levels—seen and unseen—that provides a new support system for all the plants and other life in that garden.

To sum up this first point: What nature has shown me over the years is that when we speak of nature, we are talking about everything around us. The world of nature is not just relegated to parks, farms, countryside and wilderness. It includes asphalt, high-rise apartment buildings, shopping malls and street corners.

The second important point nature is making in its definitions of form and nature is that in order for anything to be form, it must have consciousness combined with its order, organization and life vitality. This means that if you are holding some object in your hand and it has order, organization and life vitality, it must also have consciousness—otherwise, it would be beyond form and you would not be able to perceive it under any circumstances. And if it has consciousness, it has intelligence. If it has intelligence, it can communicate. If we can discover the common bridge between us for communication, we can not only communicate our ideas and thoughts to this thing in our hand, but it can also communicate its information back to us. And it has something to communicate. It knows what it is, what defines its balance, what it needs to restore and maintain that balance at any given point in time, how it fits and functions in its immediate environment and how it links with the larger picture—both on this planet and beyond.

The goal on our planet is that all consciousness reflect and flow perfectly and fully through form. This brings me to something I call "involution/evolution balance" or "i/e balance." Because nature supplies all form, and because all form has combined with it consciousness, all matter has inherent in it two dynamics: an involution dynamic that is supplied by nature and an

I/E Balance

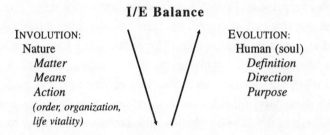

INVOLUTION:
Nature
Matter
Means
Action
(order, organization,
life vitality)

EVOLUTION:
Human (soul)
Definition
Direction
Purpose

evolution dynamic that is supplied by the consciousness. These two dynamics work in partnership, and, when left undisturbed, this partnership functions in balance. That is, the involution and evolution dynamics are fully synchronized with one another, thus creating a state of balance.

The following are three examples of i/e balance.

In this first example, evolution originates from the soul or devic level of an organism or object, and from this level definition, direction and purpose are established. When considering

A Tree's I/E Balance

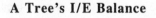

INVOLUTION:
Nature Spirit Level
Matter
Means
Action
(order, organization,
life vitality)

EVOLUTION:
Devic Level
Definition
Direction
Purpose

trees, rocks, rivers and sky—objects that we would commonly consider "nature"—nature not only supplies the order, organization and life vitality (the involution dynamic) but also the consciousness or soul (the evolution dynamic). The i/e balance is contained within nature itself. The devic level supplies the consciousness or soul input and gives to a tree its definition, direction and purpose. In fact, a good definition of the devic level is that it is that part of nature intelligence that supplies a tree's definition, direction and purpose. The nature spirit level completes the i/e balance by supplying the matter, means and action for fulfilling the goals set by the definition, direction and purpose. The devic level functions as the architect, drawing up the plans. The nature spirit level "builds" the structure according to the plans and maintains that structure throughout its full life cycle according to the patterns and rhythms set on the devic level. This is i/e balance as it is demonstrated within that area of nature. What we see functioning before us is a full reflection of form's definition, direction and purpose.

The human body provides us with another example of i/e balance. The human soul establishes the definition, direction and purpose for a specific lifetime. Nature then provides the body according to that definition, direction and purpose. The devic level creates the "blueprint" based on the soul information and the nature spirit level implements these blueprints by providing the matter, means and range of action required. The result is that this soul has the physical vehicle to fully reflect and function according to its definition, direction and purpose. Throughout the person's life cycle, the devic level modifies the makeup, patterns and rhythms according to however the person's soul modifies its original definition, direction and purpose. In other words,

The Human Body's I/E Balance

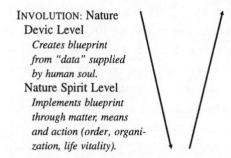

INVOLUTION: Nature
Devic Level
*Creates blueprint
from "data" supplied
by human soul.*
Nature Spirit Level
*Implements blueprint
through matter, means
and action (order, organization, life vitality).*

EVOLUTION:
Human Soul
*Definition
Direction
Purpose*

throughout a person's lifetime, there is a continuous communication between the human (evolution input) and the body's devic and nature spirit levels (involution input). A free-flowing communication between the two dynamics creates within us i/e balance and results in our having the body through which the soul may reflect and flow without constriction or interference. As a result, we experience what we call perfect health.

The glitch to our human i/e balance is free will. We can make our free will jump right into the middle of i/e balance and use it to distort our intuitive understanding of the soul's definition, direction and purpose. What if we got a glimpse of this soul information and, for whatever reason, decided we didn't like it. We wanted a different life. We perceive that the life based on the information as we understood it would be too tough or too tedious. So we insert our conscious selves right into the middle of the i/e balance and we modify that evolution information according to our preference and desire. Now nature has two sets of definitions, directions and purposes to deal with. The operating devic blueprint will still reflect the soul's original definition, direction and purpose. However, we are now consciously operating with another set of definition, direction and purpose—the free will set. As we move through our daily lives, we override the soul information with our conscious desires and we find that things are not moving too smoothly through this body. This is because we are consciously trying to move one set of evolutionary dynamics through a body that was designed for another set—the soul set. We are no longer operating within i/e balance and we will experience all kinds of health issues as a result.

Because of free will, i/e balance is a difficult dynamic for us to maintain. We frequently jump into the middle of it. For us, i/e balance rests not only on our ability to trust in the movement of our own soul, but also in our ability to consciously translate and perceive our soul's definition, direction and purpose and not use our free will to try to manipulate our soul. This is one of the things we are here on Earth to learn: the marrying of our conscious selves to our souls and the full fusion of this with our physical bodies. I am not implying that consciously achieving our i/e balance is easy. I'm only using an example that is familiar to us all in order to make i/e balance more easily understood. Well, actually, if it was just left up to our soul and nature, we would experience perfect i/e balance easily. It's free will that adds the elements of excitement, confusion and challenge. As we develop and discipline our free will, we will expand our understanding to include the wisdom to know when and how to appropriately apply free will, and our experience of i/e balance will be unencumbered and beyond words.

Another example of i/e balance is the balance that is at the heart of our co-creative partnership with nature. There are many different kinds of gardens: herb gardens, rock gardens, perennial gardens, wildflower gardens, Japanese moss gardens, Zen sand

A Garden's I/E Balance

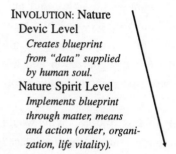

INVOLUTION: Nature
Devic Level
  *Creates blueprint
  from "data" supplied
  by human soul.*
Nature Spirit Level
  *Implements blueprint
  through matter, means
  and action (order, organization, life vitality).*

EVOLUTION:
Human
  *Definition
  Direction
  Purpose*

gardens . . . and vegetable gardens. When you are working directly in partnership with nature, you cannot simply announce, "Let's put in a garden!" and expect that you will get any information back from nature regarding the garden. You must supply the definition, direction and purpose of this garden. In other words, you must supply the evolution dynamic within the i/e balance, and you are the only one who can do it. When Peter Caddy said to me, "You are the creator of your garden" this is what he meant: Nature will not do your job for you. It will only supply the evolution dynamic for objects that fall within its "natural" domain: trees, rocks, deer, lightning, etc. It does not supply the evolution dynamic for form that falls outside this natural domain, such as gardens. Remember, gardens are a man-made invention. As soon as you are involved in its creation, you are responsible for supplying the evolution dynamic: definition, direction and purpose.

Nature creates the blueprints according to your evolution input, and it is only after this information is supplied by you that the devic level can establish the blueprint for your garden. Based on your definition (a vegetable garden), direction (a vegetable garden in my backyard that includes succession planting so that we may harvest from it as many months as possible), and purpose (a garden that feeds daily my family of six—my two teenage sons, my ten-year-old daughter, my two-year-old son, my husband and myself). It creates the order, organization and life vitality patterns and rhythms that will best respond to the information you have supplied.

Why would you go through all of this trouble? Why would you want to establish a co-creative partnership in the first place? Well, once you have supplied a good definition, direction and purpose for your garden, nature will design and implement with you a garden that will be *in balance*. And this is why you go through all that trouble. When you have balance, as in the human body, everything operates smoothly and synchronized. No more guesswork. No more trying one trick after another in order to achieve success. And the quality of food that comes from such a garden contains the same balance that is reflected in the garden.

Once we establish a co-creative partnership with nature, we have the finest experts in what needs to occur in order to achieve and maintain balance. One of the most difficult things a person new to a co-creative partnership has to learn is to not try to do nature's job. We are very used to deciding what we wish to accomplish (evolution) and then also deciding the best way to achieve our goals and the best materials to use (involution). But *equal partnership* does not mean that we are equally capable of doing nature's job. It means our role in the partnership is equal to nature's role—but the two roles are very different. When they function together equally, these two roles create a balanced partnership. The first trick to working with nature to achieve i/e balance is to do our job well and then let nature supply the matter, means and action for accomplishing the defined goal. (If this has a vague, familiar ring to you, it should. Manifestation is i/e balance in action.) At first blush, it seems like a co-creative partnership is more work than it's worth. In actuality, it takes a tremendous burden off our shoulders. People who have entered such a partnership have talked to me about the weight that has been lifted from them. They no longer have to think of everything themselves. They now have a partner who can tell them the best location for this garden, what vegetables to plant, where to plant them, what interplanting to do, when to plant, when to thin, when to water and how much . . . And all of this information has balance. This spells success.

Sometimes people assume that a co-creative relationship with nature means that they announce the definition, direction and purpose of their garden and then sit back, beer in hand, and watch nature spirits run around doing all the work. After all, I am saying that nature supplies the matter, means and action. Doesn't this mean that nature manifests the right tools and then gets out there and starts turning soil? No. It's a *working partnership*. Nature gives us the information that is needed to create this garden in balance. That includes what tools are best for achieving our goal in light of the variables, working conditions and our ability. For example, they won't suggest that your four-year-old help dig a sandbox area with a front-end loader. Nature will suggest the kind of tool that will be safe for this child to use that will also allow him a successful experience as he helps you with the digging. Nature gives you this information because it takes all the variables into account in light of your stated goal and establishes the balanced way to proceed. In short, nature doesn't do the work for you. It works with you.

I have said that there are many kinds of gardens. Some do not grow in soil. In 1993, I asked nature to define a garden.

From nature's perspective, a garden is any environment that is initiated by humans, given its purpose, definition and direction by humans, and maintained with the help of humans. For nature to consider something to be a garden, we must see humans actively involved in all three of these areas. It is the human who calls for a garden to exist. Once the call is made, nature responds accordingly to support that defined call because a garden exists through the use of form.

Humans tend to look at gardens as an expression of nature. Nature looks at gardens as an expression of humans. They are initiated, defined and maintained by humans. When humans dominate all aspects and elements of the life of the garden, we consider this environment to be human dominant. We consider an environment to be "nature friendly" when humans understand that the elements used to create gardens are form and operate best under the laws of nature, and when humans have the best intentions of trying to cooperate with what they understand these laws to be. When humans understand that nature is a full partner in the design and operation of that environment—and act on this knowledge—we consider the environment to be actively moving toward a balance between involution (nature) and evolution (human).

As a result, this last environment supports and adds to the overall health and balance of all it comprises and the larger whole. It also functions within the prevailing laws of nature (the laws of form) that govern all form on the planet and in its universe. In short, when a garden operates in a balance between involution and evolution, it is in step with the overall operating dynamics of the whole. The various parts that comprise a garden operate optimally, and the garden as a whole operates optimally.

Nature does not consider the cultivation of a plot of land as the criteria for a garden. Nature considers a garden to exist wherever humans define, initiate and interact with form to create a specialized environment. This is the underlying intent of a garden and the reason behind the development of specialized environments such as vegetable gardens. Nature applies the word "garden" to any environment that meets these criteria. It does not have to be growing in soil. It only needs to be an environment that is defined, initiated and appropriately maintained by humans.

This is what nature means when it uses the word "garden." The laws and principles that nature applies in the co-creative vegetable garden are equally applicable to any garden, whether it is growing in soil or otherwise. In order to understand why the processes described in the two Perelandra Garden Workbook*s apply to any "garden," one must understand how nature defines a garden. The principles and processes apply across the board because all gardens are operating with the same dynamics— only the specific form elements that make up each garden have changed.*

What are some of these other specialized environments or soil-less gardens? According to nature, a garden has just three criteria: It is initiated by humans, given its definition, direction and purpose by humans, and maintained with the help of humans. Well, managed forests, farms and potted plants would also be gardens that grow in soil. Soil-less gardens could include a home, large and small businesses, individual offices within a business, a classroom, a department, a college study program, a research lab, an assembly line, a car, a computer, a computer program or a human body. All of these soil-less environments meet the criteria for a garden. This is actually good news. In order to establish a co-creative partnership with nature, you won't have to give up your present life and buy land in the country. Stay right where you are. Remember, where there is form, there is nature. Where nature and humans interact, there is a garden. Where there is a garden, there is an implied co-creative partnership. And where there is a co-creative partnership, there is the potential for i/e balance.

THE LESSONS REALLY DID CONTINUE

It is important to understand that when we begin our partnership, nature communicates the information we need in a manner that makes sense to us and means something to us at the time. But, over the years, as the partnership deepens, so, too, does the breadth and depth of the information nature gives us. What we learn in the beginning is just that—a beginning. It is our starting point, and everyone has his or her own starting point. My first-year co-creative garden was my starting point, and how I perceived the events that year is the starting point of my education. Nature builds on our current understanding continuously. As we become able to work with more information, nature gives us more information.

When I first wrote *Behaving* in 1981, I had been working with nature daily for five years. I had a deep and heartfelt understanding about what I was learning and experiencing. It is with this understanding that I wrote the book. Now, sixteen years later, my understanding about nature, its role and my experiences have deepened enormously. For this edition, I debated whether I should just put aside my 1981 version of things and simply present what I understand now. But a starting point is a starting point—and *Behaving* has represented a starting point for tens of thousands of readers over the past years. As I began working on this edition, it felt right that *Behaving*'s role as an introduction to nature intelligence and the co-creative partnership should not be lost.

Part 3 is titled "The Lessons Continue," and since 1981 they have. I have continued to work with nature to learn all that I can about this amazing partnership and how it applies to the quality of our lives. I have been on this journey with nature now for over twenty years (since 1976). I've never been bored, and I've never ceased to be surprised and deeply impressed by what I learn.

I feel it is helpful to you if you not only read the "upgraded" information, but also see how later information builds on and expands from what we learn in the beginning. I have to admit to you that nature is a genius at giving us just the amount of information we can handle. I have never felt that nature has "held back" on me. To the contrary, at any given time, I have always felt that nature has stretched me about as far as I could go. Right when I'm ready to experience and learn more, nature gives me more. And all this without my demanding input from nature. I just kept my free will out of it, let nature "have its head," trusted, and this is where it has led us.

I decided to include both versions of my understanding on certain topics in this edition. By letting you read what I wrote in Part 3 in 1981 (with minor word changes that I feel make what I wrote in 1981 clearer) and what I understand about it now, I hope to show you how I've grown in understanding around these issues, how the information changes as we move through this building-block process with nature and how the information *builds* on what we know.

Nature Spirit Walkouts and a Goldfish Pond

Behaving — 1981

Unfortunately, our most prevalent relationship with nature is one of interference and manipulation. It has gotten so bad over the past fifty years that the nature spirits have, for the most part, responded by withdrawing from vast areas of land. Remember, nature spirits are responsible for the final stages of grounding energy into five-senses form and caring for the energized form throughout its various growth stages. Because of the overall ecological picture created by us, this process becomes more difficult, even impossible. As soon as a pattern is grounded, it's thrown off balance by the ecological imbalance surrounding it.

Most of the gardens and farm land around the world are now without nature spirits. Without them, the quality and amount of energy that actually grounds into form is at its minimum, allowing just enough energy for the form to remain. What we end up with is basically empty form. Food without light.

When nature spirits leave an area, they "congregate" somewhere not frequented by man, often a woods. To further discourage man from entering the area, they'll make it impassable with dead trees and overgrown vines. I experienced such an area one time. It was close to Findhorn, a piece of land and a mansion that had once been well maintained by man but then was abandoned. I was walking through the grounds and felt myself being drawn to an area away from the mansion, down a hill to a little path. As I passed through a clump of trees, I felt as if I was entering a self-contained environment that was totally different from the one in which I had been walking. The atmosphere had more of a sense of weight to it, and although I could feel peace, I could also feel anger. I considered leaving, but I was still being drawn deeper into this strange space. I walked along the path and soon found myself beside what looked to be an old goldfish pond. It was small and overgrown and totally hidden from the mansion. That's where I was contacted by the nature spirits and told what had happened and why they were there. Their anger was real, and they weren't about to leave their "sanctuary" until humans once again entered the grounds and *proved* that they were willing to work to restore the area's balance.

The nature spirits removing themselves is a serious situation that affects us directly by drastically lowering the quality of our support systems. We are constantly eating unenergized food—and it has nothing to do with the fast food chains! The next time you eat a tomato that has been grown in a commercial greenhouse, take time to look at it. Notice its square shape. Its pale coloring. Its pithy texture. And its nondescript taste. That's a perfect example of what happens to plant form when the nature spirits remove themselves from the process. It is form with minimal energy.

I don't mean to imply that nature spirits don't have the power to override a faulty, damaged and diseased environment for the sake of producing, for example, a perfect tomato plant. Of course they can do it. They proved that to me the first year we worked together. The environment in our area is full of pesticides and pollutants, and suffers from manipulative farming methods. Despite this, I saw perfection in every vegetable I planted. Each plant radiated health. But this was a special situation that was designed to give me tangible evidence of the reality to which I was opening. Under normal circumstances, nature spirits, despite their power, will simply refuse to override the effects of the environmental mess we've created. We can't stop relating to nature in imbalance unless we understand the imbalance, and we'll never get the desire to reach that understanding if our messes are constantly being cleaned up for us.

1997

The way in which I described how nature spirits withdraw from land areas and the event with nature by the old goldfish pond is exactly how I experienced and understood these things. Yet, I know more about nature and its intelligence now, and I would not explain this nature spirit phenomenon at the pond in the same way now. For one thing, I know that "deva" and "nature spirit" refer to two distinct and different levels of operation within one expansive intelligence that is called *nature intelligence*. Just recently, I asked nature to define nature intelligence.*

. . . *Nature intelligence does not include elves, faeries, gnomes and devic angels. It is a massive intelligence, a dynamic. It is not made up of individual life forms. This intelligence dynamic flows through form. It is not made up of these forms. One may look at beings such as elves and devic angels as communication bridges between man and nature intelligence. If nature is to communicate what it knows to an individual, it may create form through which this communication can flow. Nature is, after all, the order, organization and life vitality of all form. At any time, it may create, modify and utilize form in response to the moment. The "appearance" of a nature spirit is a response to the inherent balance of the moment, which includes an individual human being. More often than not, the nature-spirit form used is seen only within the mind's eye of the person with whom nature wishes to communicate. However, whether seen within the mind's eye or by the individual's outer sensory system, the form is equally real. But it is a communication bridge in the form of an elf, not an elf with an independent life of its own. The nature spirit level of nature's consciousness does not need elves and*

---

* The result of this session is a paper titled "What Is Nature Intelligence?" This paper may be obtained from Perelandra. Information for requesting our catalog is included in the Afterword.

gnomes to function. That level simply flows through all existing form directly. When such an event occurs, many humans unfortunately tend to overlay it with expectation and definition that is unique to human intelligence—rather than understand that this is a bridge from nature intelligence. It has different dynamics and has been initiated and activated for a specific purpose. If humans could focus on the communication surrounding such an event, rather than get lost in the excitement of the event itself, more would come of the experience; and it would be more useful to them, as well.

When I experienced the event by the fish pond, I had the distinct impression that I was surrounded by individualized nature spirit energies—not a dynamic, intelligence flow—and that these nature spirits had left one area, had congregated in the hidden and protected area by the pond and they were angry. In the above definition, nature tells me that my experience back then was real, but that this experience was given to me in a way that corresponded with what I understood. However, I am to focus on the communication surrounding this event if I am to understand its purpose.

Any time we humans interact with form, in this case land, we automatically create a partnership with nature. It is not usually a conscious co-creative partnership. Rather, it is a partnership based on necessity, and it is unconscious on our part. We simply cannot interact with form without also interacting with nature. The two cannot be separated. So when a farmer, for example, takes over his land he is in an immediate and implied partnership with nature. Nature looks to him to fulfill his role within i/e balance. As the farmer adds clear definition, direction and purpose to his operation, nature automatically moves to provide the appropriate blueprints and to implement these blueprints into the appropriate matter, means and action as best it can in this situation. I/e partnership isn't a new concept. Only the notion of *conscious* i/e partnership is new.

One problem right off the bat with an unconscious implied i/e partnership is that tricky free will. The farmer in this situation will take over both sides of the i/e operation and proceed to override nature's blueprint and input on the best matter, means and action for achieving his goal. When this occurs to such a degree that the farmer has willfully nullified all the input from nature, nature will respond to the situation not by going into battle with the farmer, but by "acknowledging" that this land is human-dominated and the i/e interchange between human and nature is not possible. Under these circumstances, nature intelligence will not remove itself from the land. It can't. If it did, all form that comprised that land would disappear. However, nature intelligence will maintain a minimal fusion with the makeup and continuing operation of the land because this farmer chooses to work alone. He is the creator of his own garden, and nature will not debate his decision with him.

When we sense this minimal partnership, especially after experiencing how a strong i/e partnership feels, it is a dramatic difference and we can easily believe that "nature has left." Or, the nature spirits have left. In fact, nature intelligence has simply adjusted to the will of the farmer and how he chooses to work his land.

(By the way, I don't mean to sound like I am picking on farmers. I live in farm country, and I have seen for myself some very sensitive farmers with a finely developed intuition and love of their land working in an unconscious relationship with nature.

But this is not the *conscious* co-creative partnership that I am speaking of. It is the implied i/e relationship between the farmer and nature that must occur in order for the farm to exist and to be maintained.)

At the fish pond, I experienced the difference between a strong i/e partnership (it was just after my first season of co-creative gardening) and a piece of land that had at one time been diligently pruned, clipped and mowed by a staff. It now looked abandoned and it truly felt abandoned. If nature was going to show me something about the differences between a conscious co-creative partnership and a human-dominated piece of land, I don't think it could have chosen a better experience for me. This mansion had been abandoned for many years. Its windows had all been broken by vandals, the swimming pool had a layer of sludge sitting in the bottom, its sides were all cracked and the gardens were reverting back to a wild state. But it wasn't the kind of wild state we find in the wild. There's a beauty, balance and order to the real wild. This had the appearance of chaos created by man. The combination of heavily maintained grounds while the mansion was occupied and those same grounds left completely unattended for many years created the sense of true destruction. This was the reality of that land, and it is what I was picking up as I moved through it.

I suspect that the fish pond itself had been maintained with a more responsive attitude toward nature and perhaps by a different person from those who tended the rest of the grounds. Whatever happened caused a change in that location, a stronger quality of relationship with the nature in that area which then made it easier for nature to communicate with me.

We can experience anger from nature. Emotions contain a high degree of order, organization and life vitality—all of which are supplied by nature. Emotions are form. Consequently, nature is no stranger to emotions, and this includes the emotional dynamic we call anger. But because nature does not have free will, and because it always operates with inherent balance, it will not "sit around" and choose to throw a fit like we humans. Instead, nature will automatically provide the structure and action for whatever is appropriate in any experience. The kind of destruction I witnessed on this land included anger. For example, it takes a certain degree of anger to create a comparable level of destruction. The structure and action for anger was already part of the full reality through which I was moving. It was there for me to experience just as the visual impact, the smells, the weight of the atmosphere and the sounds were there. The anger didn't originate from nature. It was part of this abandoned form that we humans created, and nature simply provided the order, organization and life vitality through which it could express. For me to understand the implications of mankind playing around with and abandoning our partnership with nature—conscious or unconscious—I had to feel the anger attached to the abandonment. So nature provided the structure that allowed me to experience the anger in a way I could understand at that time. But don't forget I also felt peace. The two emotions existed side by side and were appropriate to the situation when destruction such as this is placed within the context of the larger universal picture, which is what nature automatically does. As I said, nature provides the order, organization and life vitality for *all* the components of any defined reality or biosphere.

It was important for me to experience the differences between my garden and this abandoned land. If I was to understand what this co-creative partnership was teaching me and why it was important for me to continue with my work with nature, I needed to feel these differences. After the pond experience, there was no way I could turn back—even if I was foolish enough to consider this. The other important part of the experience was the appropriateness of the anger and how it could co-exist with peace. When we face a world that is being ravaged by mankind and even abandoned, and when we move to take our place as conscious partners with nature working together to create i/e balance, it is both hopeful and helpful to remember that anger isn't the only appropriate emotion that will be woven into the situation. So, too, is peace.

The Interplay, Intermingling and
Balancing of Energies

Behaving — 1981

The second year's garden was totally different from the first year's.

I prepared the soil carefully and went through the process of helping to ground the various vegetable energies. All was progressing beautifully—but as soon as everything was planted, I was told to do nothing more in the garden until it was time to harvest. Each day I was to walk along the garden's edge and look at the plants in each row—but I was to do nothing about what I saw. For ten weeks, I watched a disaster take place. Cabbage worms and Mexican bean beetles were all over the place. Some plants just keeled over and died. Others, like the tomato plants, went totally berserk and took over half the garden. It was a strange sight to me, especially when compared to the previous year's garden.

(Which caused a problem. We had many visitors from Findhorn the second year. All had come to see the magnificent garden I had talked about. They'd take a look at the new garden and then look at me as if I were crazy. One person even gave me the name of some gardener in Pennsylvania who I should contact, since it was obvious that I needed gardening advice. I responded to the pressure by trying to defend the garden. But instead of simply telling them that I trusted there was a reason behind what was happening, and that the reason would become clear to me once the process was completed, I tried to give them a "reasonable," logical explanation based on what I thought was happening. Of course, my conclusions were way off. But by the time I had insight into what was really going on, I had at least learned that I shouldn't let outside opinion or influence interfere with the process in my own garden.)

Actually, this second year's garden was a fact-finding mission. I was to observe what happened to the plants if left unattended once the energy was fully grounded. In essence, I saw the effect of the environment on the garden—what plants were able to maintain their strength, what plants broke down, which ones died, what insects and how many were attracted to which plants. By the end of the season, I felt like a computer, having gone through weeks of programming a vast amount of minute detail.

All those details became important once the third year's garden was started. By now, I understood quite well that my primary focus was balance and I could tell how well the balance was holding by looking at the condition of the plant. If the overall health was weak, or the color, texture and quality of fruit were off, or the plant tended to attract more insects than it could comfortably support, I knew the energy pattern or balance was being disturbed. But I didn't have the foggiest notion of how to rectify the situation—except for one thing.

Part of the patterning includes the plant's growing conditions —the climate, amount of moisture, soil texture and balance of nutrients. If I want broccoli to grow in a particular location, I have the responsibility of making sure the proper growing conditions are supplied and maintained. I've met quite a few gardeners who feel that once a person begins to work on a "higher level" with nature, they don't have to deal with mundane things such as bone meal, manure, nitrogen, lime and water. They don't realize that without the proper growing conditions, the physical aspect of the plant receives no life-sustaining support. Form is physical, and it requires other physical elements for survival. It's the same with us. We can open to our spiritual selves all we want, but if we don't bother to eat properly or if we decide not to eat at all, we get sick or we die. It's very simple.

If left alone, the broccoli would ground wherever the conditions were perfect, or nature would supply the conditions. They're quite capable of this. For example, nitrogen already exists on the planet. All nature has to do is move the energy of nitrogen, which is readily available, to a specific area and ground that energy into form, thus making it usable to the broccoli plant. But if humans are going to operate in the role as "creator of our own garden" and demand that broccoli grow in a specific area, we must then be sure that the proper conditions are met.

Once I checked the soil, water, temperature and so on, and the plant still didn't respond, I didn't know what to do. So nature started playing a little game with me that I call Cosmic Chess.

In order to achieve a more complete balance, I could no longer look at a plant or its energy as an isolated entity. I had to begin thinking of the individual in terms of its relationship with the whole. That's where the Cosmic Chess came in.

The game board was any garden at Perelandra—vegetable or flower. The first one was a small flower garden in front of the house. Mercifully, I was allowed to start small! In order to achieve balance, I had to consider the proper shape and size of the garden. I was told to mark a border that "felt right" to me, and since I wasn't sure what that meant, I simply marked a border that appealed to me. Then I was told to "feel" the energy that was now contained within that border. I still wasn't sure what I was doing, so I tried to sense something on an energy level within the border. Once completed, I was told to go away and return later that day.

When I returned, the border I had marked with timbers and a rock had moved slightly. The space was a little larger and the shape a bit different. I was told to "feel" the change. I could actually feel a change—a greater sense of stability, a smoother sensation.

The board was set. I was told to plant one plant anywhere I wished within the board, and, once it was planted, I was to feel the shift in energy. If I didn't like the feel of the energy, I could change the plant's position. Once I was happy with my "move," I was to leave and return the next day.

The next day, I found two plants in the garden—mine and a "stranger." I was told to once again feel the energy shift and that if at any time I felt nature's move created an unbalanced or uncomfortable energy for the whole, I was to correct the energy by changing their move.

We went on for a couple of weeks like this. I would make a move, then they would make a move, and each time I felt the shift in energy. As for the plants, the variety of plant and color of flower had to be considered. But we also used rocks and pieces of driftwood. With all of these, the shape, size, color and type had to be considered. Once, I placed a beautiful, large white quartz rock beside one of the plants. It shifted the entire energy balance drastically, but I thought the shift was in balance. The next day I discovered a much smaller but better quality quartz rock where mine had been. After feeling the energy, I realized that the smaller rock created a higher quality balance.

There were times when I had to "correct" a nature move— even times when my correction was re-corrected, only to have me return to correct their re-correction. I was becoming more confident about this energy thing, and they were getting more crafty with their tests. The game didn't end until I felt the garden was as balanced as it could possibly be. If I was wrong—which I was four times in the first game—I would return the next day to find a position changed, an addition made or even something removed. Once the game was called (and I was correct), we'd move to another garden and create a new board.

For the past five years, my focus with the plant kingdom has remained twofold—the individual and the whole. I work to make sure that the individual energy pattern of each plant (the devic blueprint) has the best chance of grounding and being reflected through its form. And I work to achieve the balance of the whole that I learned about through Cosmic Chess. It's a continual challenge, since atmosphere, weather and other conditions are always changing and affecting nature's balance. I'm also finding that there are levels of balance, and just as soon as I think I have everything under control, I become aware of a refinement that changes and further strengthens the entire picture.

In the spring of 1980 (my fourth year of co-creative gardening), the whole garden was shifted to a different location, and the straight rows were changed to a garden of eighteen concentric circles spaced three feet apart. (The circle as a shape is more powerful and enhances energy far better than the straight line.) The new garden is one hundred feet in diameter, has three spiral paths that meet in the center and an area for birds to feed and bathe. The fence around the garden is for the purpose of keeping out the neighbor's horses and cows, but the animals who are a part of Perelandra are free to come and go as they please. I tithe 10 percent of the vegetables and fruit back to nature, but, to be honest, I rarely notice any plant eaten or missing. Squirrels come in for their fill of birdseed. And I have a box turtle who has been part of the garden all summer, plus a few snakes—but they only *add* to the overall health. I still use no foreign repellents or insecticides, organic or otherwise. I maintain the garden on the principles of balance.

One important addition to the garden has been rocks. The very center has a 10″ x 8″ slab of clear quartz crystals sitting in the middle of a larger circle of marble chips, which is bordered by regular quartz rocks. Also near the center is a circular slate walk. All of this is to help create, stabilize, hold and enhance the overall garden energy.

1997

The point of the co-creative partnership is balance—i/e balance. Although I have not played Cosmic Chess with nature since the early years, my education about balance has been continuous. From these early exercises, I began to understand how much we humans don't understand about balance and how much we need to rely on nature's input when working to achieve it. Balance is nature's domain. In the session about nature intelligence,* nature said,

When humans consider solutions for restoring balance to an out-of-balance world, they need only access the intelligence of nature involved for answers. That intelligence contains inherent balance and is fully capable of defining all that is required for reflecting that inherent balance through specific form.

* This is an excerpt from the paper "What is Nature Intelligence?"

Playing Cosmic Chess developed my appreciation for what nature knows about balance. When my errors were corrected, I never understood why. I only knew that the chess board felt different. I learned that everything that is appropriate to the biosphere must be considered in order to achieve balance. Nothing is purely ornamental, even though it may look beautiful. I also learned that the key to balance within a specific biosphere can hinge on the addition of one final thing—a stone, an herb, a path. It can also come in some pretty unlikely ways. A co-creative gardener once told me that she didn't achieve balance in the garden one year until she placed a lawn chair between rows 3 and 4. We speculated that nature was trying to tell her that the gardener needed to rest—in the garden, between rows 3 and 4.

I am impressed with how complex this balance thing is. Since first writing *Behaving*, I have written two workbooks (the *Perelandra Garden Workbook* and the *Perelandra Garden Workbook II*) that outline and give specific processes for working with nature to get all the information needed for achieving i/e balance in a garden growing in soil or otherwise. In *Workbook II*, I introduce the concept of triangulation and balance. I won't explain the process here, but I will say that triangulation convinced me that we humans are nuts if we think we're going to figure out this balance business on our own. For example, if my green beans in row 5 are heavily infested with bean beetles all of a sudden, I might have to solve the problem by foliar feeding the beets in row 1 in a totally different section. This is because the beans in row 5 are energetically linked with the beets in row 1, and both of these vegetables are linked with the nasturtiums in row 7. The three links form a triangle that is a unit unto itself within the garden. These three points balance and stabilize one another. So, nature tells me to foliar feed the beets if I want to address the weakness with the beans. Like a good kid, I foliar feed the beets—and the next day the beans have a "comfortable" population of bean beetles. Go figure. Do I understand this beyond what I have explained to you? Of course not! On my own, I never would have come up with this answer to the bean problem. Luckily, I have nature to consult. Nature knows which plants, rocks and "things" create these special triangular units in a garden in any given year because they are part of the devic blueprint.

In 1981, I wrote that the circle as a shape is more powerful and enhances energy far better than the straight line. I know better than to say that now. Whatever shape is *the* appropriate shape for your garden, be it circle, straight line, serpentine or basket-weave, is the most powerful for you. If the information you get from nature says you should have fourteen straight-line rows within a rectangular space with a specific measurement, this is the shape that will give you the strongest energy and lead you toward balance. When I wrote that comment about circles and straight lines, I had just changed (on nature's advice) the location of my garden, its size and its shape from rectangular with straight rows to circular with eighteen concentric circular rows. The reason for the change was that I changed the intent (the evolution input) of my garden. Nature had informed me that I had an opportunity to work with them in deeper ways, thus expanding my education, and I said "yes" to it. As a result, the definition of the garden changed from a family kitchen garden for two to a cocreative research garden with a full operating laboratory. At Perelandra, in our environment, considering all the ecological variables and taking in all the variables brought into the lab by the researcher (me), the devic blueprint changed. The size and shape of the new garden, along with other changes, was what was needed to accommodate the new definition, direction and purpose.

What is important for you to understand is that whatever brings about balance in a specific biosphere is what should be considered more powerful for you than any other options. Because of the different ecological variables, the different evolution input and the different gardeners, there is no one way to lay out a garden. Even if you choose to create a research lab as I did, nature may tell you to stop thinking about my concentric circles and put in straight rows. Hopefully, I am clearing up this point of confusion: When it comes to balance, look to nature and don't pay any attention to what anyone else is doing.

One last point about my use of the term "nature spirit" in 1981. Back in the early days, I clearly felt a relationship with this level as individuated nature spirits. As I wrote in 1981, I didn't see elves and gnomes. I saw (with my outer and inner vision) energy patterns that I learned were nature spirit energy patterns. I automatically perceived my experience in ways similar to those experienced by the founders of Findhorn because I used their experiences written in the Findhorn books as my base. I don't mean to imply that this perception was wrong. I am only saying that now I understand more. If I were simply upgrading my wording in *Behaving*, I would not be leaving the impression that I was surrounded by individuated nature spirit energy. I would be writing about the nature spirit level within the vast dynamic we call nature intelligence.

The Mineral Kingdom

Behaving — 1981

I have a friend who likes to refer to numb people—extremely dense people—as people having the consciousness of a rock. Cute, but wrong. I learned during this second year that the density of the mineral kingdom relates to its power, not to a "disconnectedness" from life. It's a building power that can catalyze a sweeping shift of balance and then stabilize that shift.

Also related to rock form is another curious dynamic. The physical form of the plant—with the exception of trees and bushes—changes each year. Perennial flowers die at the end of each season only to sprout again and flourish as new plants, new form. Annuals must be reseeded. Consequently, the essence of the communication from plants tends to be in the "now," without reference to history. But minerals bridge time. They use the same form for centuries, even eons, and when we connect with that intelligence, it's quite possible for us to experience a particular historical period or event that is contained within the "cell memory" of this specific mineral. For example, a woman in one of my workshops chose to get in touch with the consciousness of a stone she had picked up on a beach in Ireland. During the meditation the stone gave her a gift—a gift of joy. To do this, it projected an idyllic beach scene where many children were playing and having a wonderful time, and the woman was enveloped with a sensation of joy which she received from the scene. But the scene wasn't contemporary. It was actually a scene that had occurred in the late 1800s on a beach in Holland—which was where this stone was sitting until being washed to the shores of Ireland.

Minerals also have a capacity to link us with other planets in the solar system. In fact, some minerals don't originate on Earth. Their vibration, originating on other planets and stars, grounds into the Earth's atmosphere and takes on five-senses form. But they never lose their connection with the place from which their vibration comes. This gives our planet a special direct link with the solar system. The emerald, for example, is not of Earth. It originates from the planet Venus. It has as part of its energy pattern the dynamic of Venus. So by connecting with the emerald's consciousness, it is possible for us to gain insights into the dynamic of Venus.

The evolutionary progression of minerals on Earth is related to *light*. They begin in the ground in darkness and gradually surface to take on the sun's light. Many, as they evolve, become less cloudy. This allows light to enter and move through the minerals. I am told by nature that eventually minerals will be clear and radiate their own light from their center, rather than taking on light from an outside source.

Just as we can place a rock in a garden and have the energy field dramatically shift, we can experience the same by wearing gems. Each mineral has contained within its pattern qualities and characteristics that, when added to our own energy field, can enhance and even heal us by restoring us to our balance. For example, amber* enhances physical strength and stamina, and I have worn a piece when I felt my own stamina would be taxed. The properties from the amber commingle with my energy field and add to my field a specific dynamic that enhances my physical strength and stamina.

The easiest way for us to know what stones we should wear and when is by following our intuition. If, after wearing it for awhile, we feel like all we want to do is take it off and put it away, it most likely means we no longer need it—until we get the desire to put it on again. It sounds simple. All we're doing is reacting to the effect of the stone's energy on our own. Our natural response is to feel comfortable with or actually desire to have near us the stone whose energy happens to fulfill a particular balancing need. Or, if the energy of the stone is grating to our energy, our natural response is to back away—remove it from our field. Even if we don't consciously feel the grating or abrasive quality that the stone creates, we register it unconsciously and we'll move away from it. All we have to do is teach ourselves not to interfere with this intuitive process, which we do so easily when we tell ourselves that such reactions are silly and should be ignored.

---

* Strictly speaking, amber is not a mineral. It is a hard fossil resin. It is often listed with minerals and it impacts our energy field in ways that are similar to minerals.

1997

One of the things I've noticed over the years about our personal relationship with minerals and gemstones is that we allow our intellect to guide what we wear or carry around. Somewhere along the line we read or hear about different properties the stones contain and we decide these properties may help us feel better, so we wear the stone. In the example above, amber is known to enhance physical strength and stamina. This may be so, but does amber enhance the *specific* kind of strength and stamina you need at a specific time? And, if so, does this mean that you need to wear amber constantly? Or is it better to wear it for just a certain period each day? Or every other day? Is all amber alike in its effects, no matter what size and color? Will wearing a stone on your finger give you the same effect as wearing it around your neck or wrist? If not, what is the best location for you to wear a specific stone?

The human body is a garden, and as good co-creative gardeners we wouldn't arbitrarily decide our garden needs a certain stone we happen to like and plunk it where we think it would look best. If this were the case, why would nature have put me through all those Cosmic Chess lessons? If we would like to wear stones, it would be good to consider wearing the ones that enhance our balance, rather than those that add properties we don't need and, therefore detract from our balance. Intuition is certainly a good way for us to discern which stones are appropriate for us to wear and when. But intuition is often difficult to accurately discern, and it is easily overridden by personal preferences and desires. I recommend using the tool of kinesiology (muscle testing) to discern which stones are best for you and when. Kinesiology bypasses intellect and desire, and, from the test results, you'll know what stones enhance your balance and how best to use them. The steps for learning to use kinesiology and working with nature to get the information are contained in the *Perelandra Garden Workbook.*

Sometimes I liken the work it takes to achieve balance in something to making a complex, fine gourmet soup. We don't just stand before an empty vat, throw in all the ingredients and boil the contents like crazy for a couple of hours. A good soup is "constructed" slowly. We add the first ingredients carefully and in the correct order. Then we simmer for a while and carefully add more ingredients. We continue this process until all the ingredients have melded and we have a fine soup with all kinds of subtle tastes. Usually there is one last step in the recipe: Add salt to taste. If we get at all heavy handed about this, we will lose the delicate flavors we have worked to achieve and salt will dominate the taste. In effect, the soup will have fallen apart.

I tend to think of this analogy most when I see people who are obviously heavy handed when it comes to wearing stones. They have chosen the clothes they are wearing with some thought and care. Then they place stoned jewelry on every digit and hang more from every spare piece of available flesh. When they walk by, I can feel that this is just too much salt—way too much salt. Then there are those (usually women) who heard about amber enhancing physical stamina and strength and have apparently decided you can never have too much stamina and strength. So they put on an amber necklace that looks like it weighs about thirty pounds. It takes stamina and strength just to haul one of those babies around.

In short, minerals assist us greatly both personally and in our environment. But, as with everything else, they need to be used well. There is such a thing as too many stones. If we believe that minerals have the power to introduce certain properties needed for our bodies and environment, then it is reasonable to consider that too much of a good thing may lead to imbalance. We have over-salted the situation. I strongly urge you to work with nature when adding or taking away minerals from any garden, be it in soil or not.

The Animal Kingdom

Behaving — **1981**

The animal kingdom is so different from the plant and mineral kingdoms in dynamics and energy that, when I first connected with its essence through the gateway of the wild animals at Perelandra, I had to keep reminding myself that I was still working with nature.

The principal dynamics to which animals are responding are individuation and the expression of that individuation. We see this demonstrated primarily on the level of emotions. Unlike the other two kingdoms, they utilize the reincarnation principle as we know it—they live multiple lifetimes in order to move through their evolutionary process. They often begin as part of a group soul that we see as herds of wild animals. Eventually, they may break away from the pack concept and move into experiencing life as an individual, either in a smaller pack with highly evolved interactions (wolves, elephants, orangutans, etc.) or as a loner. After this, they may move into a relationship with man either as a wild animal interfacing with man or as the companion animal living with man, for it is through the animal's interrelationship with humans that he can fine-tune certain areas of his ability to express and communicate as individuals.

The animal kingdom serves both the planet and mankind as a buffer. Animals are very receptive to the many different energies moving through our Earth's atmosphere. They respond to those energies accordingly and function much like shock absorbers by absorbing them, thus buffering us and the planet from the intensity that is present in these energies. That's what is happening when we see animals suddenly act differently or strangely for no apparent reason—baying, howling, restlessness, and so forth.

Also as part of their buffering service, animals absorb and, to a limited degree, transmute human projections and imbalances on an emotional level. Our lives would be much harsher, more difficult physically, were it not for the animal kingdom functioning as a sheath around us and working with us on unconscious levels. The wild animals absorb the imbalanced energy of massive group actions such as war, famine, poverty and mass death. The animals who are more in touch with individual humans interact with the emotionally imbalanced environment around that human.

We are just beginning to learn what it is to express our emotions in a full and appropriate manner—that is, how to responsibly and effectively act in a charged or stressed situation. If we simply let off steam and don't take responsibility to act on, change or complete the situation in question, we do nothing more than discharge emotional energy in its raw form. If an animal is part of the environment (as a companion), it will automatically respond to this raw energy, thus becoming the buffer between us and the energy. Sometimes it will move the energy through its body via action. Dogs and cats, for example, will absorb the raw emotional energy that is released during an argument and then act on it by coming to the people involved and insisting on attention —kind, caring attention—something the people arguing needed of do for themselves. Other times, a companion animal will respond to what it's absorbing by simply reflecting the emotion in its own behavior—withdrawing inside itself, showing hurt and distrust, getting manic, whining, jumping around. None of these reactions is in response to something that's happened to the animal directly but rather to the emotionally charged energy that's flying around the room.

We need to be mindful of this service that animals unconsciously perform for us. If we're having an argument while an animal is in the room, it would be good to be aware of the animal's presence and remove it from the immediate environment if it looks as if the argument is going to be lengthy or especially intense. After the argument, whether the animal's been removed or not, make it a point to spend some time stroking and soothing it. (If you have any doubts about animals functioning in this way, watch their reactions during and just after an argument—or during a period of emotional crisis. Observe how their daily patterns change.) Another thing we can do as part of our co-creative partnership with animals is to include them in our visualization when we do the Energy Cleansing Process, which is included in Part 4 of this book.

Here is a special note to people who work in health-related areas and who include animals in the work environment. Some companion animals have the tendency to be drawn into a therapy or examination room and will automatically absorb energy that is released from the person while the work is being done. I've had massage therapists tell me that their cat will jump up and settle *on* the person during the session. If we aren't mindful of what the cat is doing, we run the risk of letting it take on too much, client after different client, day after day. As homey as the cat desiring to be close by may appear, it would be best to frequently remove it from the room. If an animal takes on too much, its system will stress and, with enough stress, it will get sick and possibly die. A daily use of the Energy Cleansing Process would be more appropriate than depending on our companions to take on everything for us.

Animals will not be able to fully learn how to express and communicate emotionally as individuals until they no longer have to serve as buffers of our emotions. So, once again, we see that it is vitally important that humans continue to learn about our emotional level and become masters of it. Much with us and around us depends on this.

To evolve toward individuation does not mean that animals look to us to remake them in the image of ourselves, as little extensions of us. So often, people force themselves on animals to such a degree that the personality of the animal no longer exists. Instead, there is the personality of a little, somewhat furry, human. In an animal/human relationship, humans are meant to enter into a partnership. They are in a co-creative relationship, each party adjusting to and accommodating the other party—not just the animal adjusting to the human and his environment. The personality of the animal needs to remain intact.

As for the issue of meat eating: To eat or not to eat meat. There are two issues here: (1) Should humans eat meat? and (2) Should humans kill animals? We tend to blend these two issues and get ourselves on an emotional treadmill. I'll address each issue separately.

Should humans eat meat? All form on Earth is physically sustained by the elements of nature—and that includes us. Our ability to fully ground and reflect our soul through five-senses form is intimately linked to how close we are to achieving and maintaining physical balance. The quality of the physical must correspond to the quality of soul reflection. A lesser physical body will simply not be able to support the amount of soul action, and the soul energy will be blocked.

The physical quality of our form depends on our achieving and maintaining the correct balance among all the various elements that go into sustaining us. Everyone's balance is different. And everyone's balance changes as they go through different stages. Not only is there no one hard set of rules that can totally achieve physical balance for any group of people, there's no one hard set of rules for any one person. We simply have to approach this whole area of physical balance with intelligence, discovery and *flexibility.*

When I questioned nature about what it was like for the plants in the garden to be cut and eaten, I was told that this was part of the plants' service to man, the support and sustenance of his physical form. The life cycle of the plant wasn't ended at harvest—it continued through preparation and eating, until the plant life cycle became an integral part of the human life cycle. Nature celebrates in this special relationship between man and itself.

I was also told—and have heard the same from other sources —that eventually humans will not need to eat meat for their balance. But we are now in a period of transition, and as a whole we have not reached the point where we no longer need animal protein. Nature has suggested that our animal intake focus more on fish and fowl. Certainly this is being verified by the recommendations of the medical establishment that we eat more fish and fowl, less beef and pork.

The upshot to the question about whether or not we should eat meat is that probably most of us should. How much or how little depends on each of us individually. Each of us has to seek out our own balance and find what amount of meat enhances our life rather than takes away from it.

I've met vegetarians who look as if they should be in a hospital. Their bodies were completely shot, and they weren't able to express one clear, insightful statement if their lives had depended on it. Instead, they were crabby, sluggish, dour, sour, numb or downright sad. I have also met a few vegetarians who radiated health, joy and wholeness. I was a vegetarian for the first five years after I moved to Perelandra. It was an appropriate response to that particular period in my life. Now, I have included some meat, fowl and fish in my diet—another appropriate move. Had I not responded to the changes that have taken place in my life and had I insisted on maintaining one diet no matter what, I would have thrown my physical balance way off and made my inner changes and growth that much more difficult.

There is one other issue surrounding the question of whether or not we should eat meat—that's the issue of the psychological pressures, even violence, we direct at one another over this issue. During one of my workshops, we got into a rather lengthy discussion over this point. Most of the people had either visited or been members of communities that honored only the vegetarian diet. If the person expected to be welcomed in the community, he'd better not eat meat. If the community was primarily vegetarian but tolerated the eating of meat by those who felt they needed it, the meat-eater got another form of pressure. Basically, he was treated like a mass murderer. People wouldn't sit at his table. Snide remarks were made as others walked by. In subsequent spiritual discussions, it was assumed that he would be less spiritually aware. I sometimes feel that vegetarianism has become to the New Age movement what getting arrested was to the antiwar movement—a badge solely designed to show others that we are seriously committed to the cause.

Balance is a complex matter. What do our systems, our glands, organs, bones, muscles and skin need in order to function *properly*? To learn this for ourselves is an educational process in itself. Other than sharing what we have learned in our own quest, I feel we have no right to impose on others what we understand to be our own response to physical balance.

Should we kill animals? If some of us still need meat, then we have to kill animals. But we need to learn what must be done to make this process responsible and balanced. Our present system of slaughtering could use improvement.

This is what I have learned about a new process. We need to understand that the animal kingdom, as well as the plant and mineral kingdoms, automatically participates in the life process of all form—including mankind. Once we understand the relationship between us and animals, we can work co-creatively to develop livestock management and slaughtering processes that reflect balance. The responsible cattleman will be the person who puts out the call to the Overlighting Deva of Cattle (defines his intent to establish and maintain a herd of cattle to eventually serve as food for humans) and will draw to himself the herd which responds to this specific service to man. So just as the intent in the vegetable garden has always clearly included using the vegetables to feed ourselves, the same will be true in the animal kingdom. To understand this more fully, we must remember that the life process doesn't end with the "harvest." There is not death —only transition. But by our having clear intent, we allow those in the animal kingdom to appropriately respond to our intent.

As to the actual slaughtering process, I haven't participated in the slaughter of livestock. I don't know if I ever will. But I feel that as we develop our understanding toward the forms of slaughter that are in balance with the animals' death process, we'll find that the more highly trained people in death-transition will be doing this work.

I have, however, been directly involved with the death-transition process with animals when they've passed over due to illness or injury. I had to go through a lot of growth and development to get to the point where I could be present during death and not feel pity, pain or revulsion. When I first came to Perelandra, I would practically pass out every time a cat got a mouse. Gradually (and gently), nature gave me experiences designed to lift me out of what I eventually saw to be reactions that only complicated, disturbed, distorted and added pain to the death process. Finally (after three years!), I got to the point where I could see an animal dying, acknowledge his sacred dance of death, respond (if needed) and maintain my focus on the animal with an attitude of appreciation and support throughout the entire process. With this, I became a positive participant rather than someone who complicates life and compromises balance.

As soon as I reached this point, I had opportunities to hold animals while they went through their death process. What I felt —actually *felt* with my hands—was the instant the soul separated from the body. The animals didn't have the sentimental attachment to their bodies that we have and easily separated their soul dynamic from the form. Just a moment before the separation, they gathered in all of their physical energy and used this energy to go into a short, frantic, full-strength convulsion, at the end of which their soul "popped" free of the body. At the same time, the eyes glassed over. The heart was still beating. The lungs even continued to work. I held the body until it became calm and still. At the same time, I asked the overlighting deva of the animal to assist the soul through the remainder of its transition process. Afterwards, I was always left with a feeling of wholeness and a special intimacy toward the animal about what I had experienced.

1997

I've learned a lot more about animals since 1981. Let me begin by first letting you read what nature has to say about the animal kingdom in the session on nature intelligence.

We would like to address the animal kingdom, for it is this area of nature where nature intelligence expresses itself most closely with human intelligence. Notice we said "expresses itself most closely," and did not say that the two intelligences were related or identical in any way. Within the animal kingdom the underlying dynamic of intelligence is still inherent balance. Often this is demonstrated through instinct. Animals act on instinct. The fact that the animal kingdom includes brains, central nervous systems and sensory systems does not mean that it functions with free will. It does mean, however, that animals, because they have similar means of receiving and expressing stimuli, are more able to communicate what they know directly with humans in a way that is similar or familiar to humans. Oak trees simply do not have the direct, five senses for communicating with humans that a wolf or cat does. In short, oak trees don't have lips.

An animal may express what it knows at any given moment through its sensory system. It also receives information about what is presently going on in its environment through its sensory system. Consequently, an individual may understand what an animal knows through its eyes, its touch, its sounds. This does not mean an animal has intelligence traits identical to human traits simply because it can express what it knows through its eyes. Animals do not think, consider, debate, believe, daydream, understand, define or hypothesize. They don't need to. They know, and what they know is based on inherent balance and is expressed instinctually.

Animals that closely interface with humans (companion animals) also operate according to inherent balance. However, their environment and daily rhythms are defined by humans. Their instincts are expressed, but within the context of a human world.

When there is a successful relationship between human and animal, the individual provides the environment and daily rhythm that takes into consideration and best suits the animal's ability to reflect inherent balance within the context of the individual's defined environment. In short, the two very different needs are expressed within one environment that is provided by man. (Conversely, in the wild, the animal provides the environment's operating "rules" for animals that the human adjusts to.) When the relationship between man and companion animal is not successful, man has provided an environment that is to his own liking but does not allow the animal to express inherent balance. The animal's daily rhythms are defined and dictated solely by the individual, and the animal often expresses behavior appropriate to the situation that humans call "neurotic."

It is important that man understand that the differences between human and nature intelligence remain the same when referring to animals. Animals are not creatures with one foot in the nature world and one foot in the human world. When an individual confuses this issue and looks at animals as furred or feathered humans, he misses the opportunity to interface with nature intelligence through form with a brain, central nervous system and sensory system that are similar to his own. This similarity enables humans to experience nature intelligence more easily. The similar physical makeup between man and animal doesn't mean the intelligences are similar. It only means that some of the ways of expressing the respective intelligences are similar.

People with companion animals may say that their animals have the ability to argue, observe, educate, decide and understand—all aspects of human intelligence. A fight to establish or maintain dominance does not equate with the criteria of a human argument. The ability to see does not equate with the ability to observe. Evolutionary development based on opportunities presented in an animal's environment and survival instincts do not equate with education. Acting on instinct does not equate with the ability to make decisions. And knowing that is based on inherent balance does not equate with understanding. With each intellectual trait individuals observe in animals that appears similar to human intellectual traits, they must view the animal trait from the perspective of inherent balance and the human trait from the perspective of free will. Only then will humans begin to understand the true differences between the traits and how they are expressed. And it is then that humans will begin to learn and understand something about the intelligence, which is so different from their own, that is called "nature intelligence."

In 1981, I wrote in *Behaving*: "Unlike plants, but like man, animals are not of Earth. They are souls from outside Earth who have chosen to use this planet as an evolutionary experience. But rather than participate in the Earth experience in its most complex manner, they participate through nature—more specifically, the animal kingdom. They are not lesser than we. They are simply different." At the time, I firmly believed that form as we know it (five-senses form) was experienced only on Earth. Nature didn't tell me anything like this. I picked up the information from others around me and, at the time, it made sense. So it became part of my belief system. Since then, I've learned from nature that five-senses form as we know it is demonstrated on many different levels and dimensions throughout reality. (If you wish to know more about my lessons and experiences in this area, I recommend *Dancing in the Shadows of the Moon.*) What I understood about the origin of animals in 1981 fit into my belief system back then. I didn't know that there were many different levels of form, all of which include nature and some of which reflect nature as we know it on Earth. Nature "nudged" me to expand by picking the one area I was most willing to believe might have some link similar to our own beyond Earth—animals. Why was I more willing to believe that animals could be a part of reality beyond Earth? Because I observed similarities between the makeup and actions of human and animals, and I equated them more than I realized. I knew that we humans could experience life beyond Earth and I assumed the same was true for animals. This was the door to the larger understanding that I had ajar, and nature took advantage of it. What I did not understand until later was that the soul dynamics of some plants could also originate beyond Earth, and some animals could originate on our planet as well as beyond Earth. Those lessons continue!

Since childhood, I have recognized that animals express emotions and that I could figure out what was being expressed. I also saw that the many companion animals in my life could read my emotions—and pretty darn accurately, too. It was part of the magic I always felt when I was around animals. I realize now that animals express *all* elements of nature intelligence.* But, unlike a plant, an animal has the physical vehicle for expressing nature intelligence in ways that we can more easily understand and learn from. Because I was so sensitive from childhood on to the emotional aspect of animal expression, this is where nature began its lessons as to what animals are and how they fit into the larger picture.

There is no question that animals respond to and express emotions. Doing this well is part of the individuation process on which they are focused. However, *all* of nature responds to and can express emotions. It's just that emotional expression for a cucumber is going to appear quite subtle to us—so subtle that we won't perceive it. A cucumber simply does not have the physical facility for expressing in a way that we humans can perceive. And the aspects of any given emotion that are expressed will be appropriate to a cucumber. We may barely recognize an emotion

* Homo sapiens are sometimes listed in science as animals. But because of the differences between nature intelligence and human intelligence, we are not animals. We are humans, and we can express all elements of the vast dynamic of human intelligence. We do not express animal intelligence. For a better understanding of this, I recommend the paper "What Is Nature Intelligence?" See the Afterword for information about how to receive our catalog.

214

when expressed within the range of a cucumber. In short, a cucumber's expression of anger may be different from anything we have experienced or know about anger. Yet a cucumber's expression of anger is still very much a part of what constitutes anger.

But another important point is that we mustn't get all caught up in this notion of expression. Don't assume we know all there is to know about expressing. We only know *something* about what it is to express through form that is like ours. Remember when I described my experiences of feeling anger and peace at the abandoned goldfish pond? I was experiencing an expression of emotion from nature. A tree didn't suddenly start jumping around and screaming at me. Both of these emotions were simply part of the reality of this defined space (the abandoned mansion and grounds), and nature provided the means for me to experience it. This is just one way nature can express emotion and an example of how much we still have to learn about the concept of expressing.

I've learned from nature that all experience includes physical dynamics, emotional dynamics, mental or intellectual dynamics and soul dynamics. Think about this. What nature is saying truly expands the definition of experience. All experiences, whether humans create them or not, contain *all* four of these dynamics. They are a natural part of experience. We perceive only that degree of any given experience that our sensory system can handle. The bottom line: There's a lot more going on that we don't perceive. However, it is not more than nature "perceives" because nature is "required" to provide the order, organization and life vitality for all four levels of this experience swirling around us, and that includes expression. Nature *is* the full expression of all experience because it not only provides the structure and action needed for expression on the four levels, it is the structure and action of that expression. Remember, nature said it not only *provides* all order, organization and life vitality for all form, it *is* form's order, organization and life vitality. Consequently, nature is intimately involved in all experiences and the expression of all the dynamics contained in all experiences.

So, since 1981 I have learned that all of nature responds to and experiences emotions, not just animals. Because of free will, we humans can create emotions. They become part of the environment of which we are a part when we create the emotion. This means that all the form around us responds to the emotions that we introduce into its environment. Now, we are much better at recognizing and reading an animal's responses to emotions than we are a chair's or plant's or rock's. Therefore, we can use this situation to our advantage and consider an animal's responses as a barometer for what is happening in that environment—and do something about it. A sudden change in an animal's behavior is telling us that something is out of balance and everything in this environment is also being affected. Because the animal can express in ways that are familiar to us, we can not only pick up from them that something is wrong, but sometimes we can look at how they are acting and accurately perceive what emotional release is causing the imbalance. This can give us clues about the problem so that we can act to restore balance to our environment.

In 1981, I recommended that we take charge of this situation by using the Energy Cleansing Process in our home and business environment regularly. I still recommend this, and the steps for this process are included in Part 4. Since then, we have developed other tools for addressing the situation: environmental balancing using processes included in the two *Perelandra Garden Workbooks* such as the Battle Energy Release Process, the Balancing and Stabilizing Process and the various processes using the Perelandra Essences. And we may work with a special environmental balancing in the Perelandra Microbial Balancing Program (see the *Perelandra Microbial Balancing Program Manual*).

Since the publication of *Behaving*, the most vitriolic letters I've received (by far, these letters were in the minority) have been from vegetarians who take issue with me about my stand on our eating meat. I maintain this stand. Here's my point: We are each responsible for providing whatever it takes to create balance within our bodies. For some people, that includes eating meat. For others, it doesn't. About the only other thing I want to say about this is *folks, calm down and get a grip.* It's hard enough to figure out this balance business for ourselves. And as soon as we feel we have a handle on it, our variables change and we have to work toward a new balance. In light of this, it's pretty goofy to presume we know what another person needs for his or her balance.

There is an obvious problem for some about equating a head of broccoli with a lamb or steer. I have learned from nature that life is life and, as far as nature is concerned, life is not rated on a sliding scale. The life of a broccoli head is no less than the life of a lamb. It's just that broccoli heads don't have soft brown eyes and nuzzle up to us. Nor do they romp and play in fields and make sweet sounds. Since the life of a broccoli plant is no less

217

than that of a lamb's, we need to treat the broccoli with appropriate respect also. And since the life of the lamb is no greater than that of a broccoli's, we need to include broccoli *and* lamb appropriately in our diet and not exclude either food source because of our misguided "respect."

This brings me to the issue of how we kill animals for our consumption. Slaughtering as it is set up now is unquestionably barbaric—for animals and the humans who have to do it. The point is this: If we need to eat meat for our balance, and we have this intimate relationship with all the kingdoms of nature when addressing our personal health and physical maintenance, then there are answers to how to move animals through their death process that will reflect balance for the animals and humans involved. Recently, there have been improvements made to the systems designed to lessen stress for the animals. But this is just a beginning. Nature holds the answers. Remember what nature has said: *When humans consider solutions for restoring balance to an out-of-balance world, they need only access the intelligence of nature involved for answers. That intelligence contains inherent balance and is fully capable of defining all that is required for reflecting that inherent balance through specific form.* Hopefully, people working in this area will soon learn about co-creative partnerships and how to work with nature directly to set up the different systems needed for slaughtering that will reflect i/e balance. Nature will not "suggest" systems that do not address the appropriate well-being of the animals or humans involved. In short, the co-creative systems will strike a balance that addresses both the humans' needs and the animals' needs.

AND FINALLY . . .

All universal truths are available to us. All universal knowledge. Everything that is, is there for us to know. Nothing is withheld. Our soul has a limitless capacity to enfold and know all. This is part of the dynamic of the soul. But when we chose to experience life on Earth, we chose to learn what it is to reflect this vast reservoir of knowledge through the tool we call our physical body.

If we allowed all knowledge from our soul level to fully flow and be totally accessible to our conscious self, the self operating in the body, before we disciplined ourselves on how to respond to such a flow on the physical level, we would shatter. Blindly expressing limitlessness through limitation would be more pressure than our bodies could bear.

So we've set up a safety valve—or more accurately, we've developed a safety screen. The screen allows through only as much knowledge as we can safely handle on our present physical level. What we filter through is what we call reality. We ground that reality through our body, reflect it from within to outside via action, thus creating the environment around us that conforms to and verifies our inner reality. For example, if you placed a single rose before ten people and asked them to write about what they saw, you probably would get ten totally different answers. Each person would see something different, something that corresponded to his inner sense of reality about the rose.

As we learn more about how to get the soul and the physical body to function together, the opening of our screen expands to allow in more of the universal reality. This results in our personal reality changing, and our environment changes to accommodate our new way of "seeing." We grow, the screen shifts, our reality changes, our environment shifts. A chain reaction occurs. Then we start growing again. . . .

Each reality we hold is truth—an aspect of the truth, part of the universal reality. Enfolding more into our consciousness doesn't mean that our old reality becomes less truthful. It simply means that our new reality is a more appropriate truth—we have expanded to take in more aspects of the universal reality. To say that the single rose is a flower is no less truthful than talking for twenty minutes about the many different properties of the rose. The twenty minutes is an expansion on the reality that the rose is a flower.

Also, the more our conscious reality expands, the more available our environment is to us. Saying the rose is a flower allows us limited access into the essence of the rose. But to talk for twenty minutes about the rose's properties gives us far more accessibility to the greater essence of the rose. We take in from an object, a person or a plant what we have already allowed into our conscious reality. For example, say a woman believes that everyone is "out to get her." That's her reality. It's one, small aspect of the vast truth about humanity. When she meets people, all she sees and all she draws from them are actions designed "to get" her. All other aspects about humanity are screened from her by herself, and they won't be available to her until she broadens her personal reality to take in more of the universal reality of humanity. Even if vast displays of love and caring are occurring around her, she won't be able to see them because she has made no place in her consciousness for those things to register.

Here is another example, this time extended to include a garden: We eat food. Our physical body needs food in order to be sustained. The quality of food we take in depends on two things: (1) how and with what consciousness the food is grown and (2) the scope of our reality regarding nature. Let's say I give two people each a cantaloupe that has been grown in the Perelandra garden. One person thinks that nature is nice but is here as a servant to man. The other person understands that we are equal partners with nature, that there is higher intelligence within nature, and we must conduct our lives from within a co-creative partnership. Both people are going to take in a higher quality of food simply because the cantaloupes were grown with an expanded sense of care and contain a high degree of balance. But the fuller reality of the cantaloupe will be less available to the first person because of the limitations in the scope of his personal reality regarding nature. Of course, nutrients from the cantaloupe will be taken in by him but not nearly the range of quality of those nutrients as are taken in by the second person. That's how much control we have on our personal reality.

In order for the soul and body to function within i/e balance, the quality of the body must be on a comparable level with the soul quality flowing through it. Otherwise, the body won't be able to support the more intense reflection of the soul, and the person will have difficulty functioning. As has been stated earlier, the makeup of our body comes from nature, which supplies the order, organization and life vitality that is defined by our soul. However, the quality of our body is also intimately linked with our conscious awareness of nature—and this bears directly on the balance between body and soul. If we strive to function as fully conscious ensouled beings, we must also expand our understanding of nature in order to be able to take full advantage of the physical vehicle that has been defined by our soul and provided for us by nature. In this situation, what we are willing to perceive about nature and its role regarding our body directly affects how much we are physically available to ourselves. In short,

we are the creators of our own garden—consciously and unconsciously.

And finally—we are faced with the job of healing the planet, healing it from the multitude of messes we have created. Once we open to the concept of nature intelligence, the reality of energy behind form and the consciousness contained in that energy—once we open to all of this, we begin to see the depth of the consequences of our old attitudes.

I realize that this may seem overwhelming or, at the very least, intense. But it's important that we consider the scope of what is involved here. We're talking about the healing of a planet. We're also talking about the quality of physical survival—of ourselves and everything around us.

Two movements of people are needed: One is the activists, the movers and shakers, those people who dedicate their time and energy to co-creative research, teaching and working as professionals to restore nature to its balance.

The other movement involves everyone. In order for the co-creative activists to be effective, the general flow of ecological destruction has to stop. The only way that can happen is for people to change their attitudes toward nature. As we each open to the broader reality of nature, our attitudes will automatically shift, and how we treat our immediate environment will alter to accommodate those shifts in attitude. We will live our lives differently. We will have different motivations for what we do. We will become active co-creative partners in life. We will behave as if the God in *all* life mattered.

The co-creative activists alone can't reverse the flow of ecological destruction. This has to be done by everyone. Each person who shifts his attitude, who accepts nature as an equal partner and who responds to and works within this partnership will create one more space that is moving toward i/e balance.

That, my friends, is how Earth will ultimately be healed.

4

I Can Do It Myself, Ma!

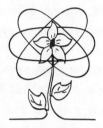

So, HOW DO WE GET STARTED? How do we begin the process of changing our attitudes, of integrating a new reality? How do we respond to and work with this equal partnership we were meant to have with nature?

Well, one way is to do what I did. It's quite simple: Just say, "I want this in my life," explain what you mean by "this" and ask nature for help. Then be quiet and listen. Whatever comes to mind, whatever springs up for you intuitively, don't dismiss it. Act on it. No matter what. No matter how weird it may sound to you. If it's an insight or a flash rather than something you can act on, write it down. It's very important that some action be taken, because this is the sign to nature that you're serious. Then be quiet again, listen and act. . . . Be quiet, listen, act. . . .

The process is started. All you have to do is keep listening, keep acting and hang onto your socks—you're in for the time of your life!

Now, we all know that for anything to be valid, it can't apply only to one situation or one thing. And we all know that every reader isn't going to buy a shovel and a handful of vegetable seed packets and head out of his or her apartment in search of a plot of land just sitting there waiting for him or her to start a garden. Not everyone is meant to create a Perelandra—that would be a bit foolish. But everything that happens at Perelandra can be re-created in any other environment—and that does need to happen. Remember, the Perelandra garden is but one window to i/e balance and universal truth. The same balance and truth are available to each of us through our own individual windows. Remember that a garden is initiated by humans, given its definition, direction and purpose by humans and maintained with the help of humans. So if sweating and getting grimy fingernails isn't your route, pick your own garden in which to work with nature. I offer these last pages to you as an aid to getting started in your own environment. I include reminders from the previous chapters of the general concepts we're working with, plus some easy exercises you can do for yourself to experience the energy behind form and how it affects your immediate environment. I also include an important process (the Simplified Energy Cleansing Process) that is designed to help you get your environment cleansed, clear and moving toward balance. I've tried to offer as many suggestions, aids and hints as I can think of to help you through the exercises with ease.

"INANIMATE" OBJECTS AND ENERGY

An important thing to remember about energy: All energy has contained within it intelligent consciousness. It knows what it's doing and why, and it knows its relationship in the scheme of things. And if we choose and are willing to expand our understanding of communication, that information is available to us. All that is around us is participating in this thing we call intelligent life, and we only fool ourselves when we think that humans are the only participants on Earth. The word "inanimate" refers to a type of form, not to the quality of intelligent consciousness contained within that form.

In order to experience the effects of the energy in inanimate objects, we can duplicate in a room what I experience in the garden by playing a variation of Cosmic Chess. So, choose a room —any room where you live. I suggest a small room so that the experiment won't become unmanageable. (But if you've got this sudden hankering to undertake a big room, be my guest.)

Cosmic Chess Exercise

1. Enter the room, sit anywhere, close your eyes and become very calm. When you're as calm as possible, allow yourself to become aware of the room. Keep your eyes closed. Feel the room. (If you don't understand "feel," just do what I did and guess at it. The concept of feeling becomes clearer as you continue and have something with which to compare it.)

2. Get brave and gutsy, and totally mess up the room. Change the position of things. Take items off tables and place them on the floor. Spread paper all around. Remove cushions. Tip chairs and tables—carefully. (I don't mean a wreck, I mean a mess.) Use your creativity and mess up the room as much as possible. When finished, sit down in the same place you sat before, get quiet again and, with your eyes closed, feel the difference in the room. (If you have difficulty getting quiet again, don't think you're failing at this. You're most likely sensing the disturbed energy so much that it's making it impossible to achieve inner quiet.)

3. Straighten the room back to its original condition. Sit in the same place and, once again, feel the difference. Then move quietly to other places in the room, one place at a time, stopping at

each, closing your eyes, getting calm. Sense the room from the new vantage point and see if there is a difference. Each time you make a move, spend a moment getting calm again with your eyes closed before you attempt to sense the energy. (Closing your eyes removes visual distractions.)

4. Change the room around—rearrange it into a new pattern, one that's pleasing and neat. Return to your original place in the room, get quiet and sense the change. Feel how the energy has shifted.

5. If you have a strong sense of the energy shifting in the room, try something a bit more subtle. Choose one item and change its position in the room. Don't just move it from one end of a table to the other—change it to the other side of the room. Feel the room again (from your original position) and notice the change that moving one item has made in the room. Then choose the same item and remove it from the room. Take it at least five feet away from the outside perimeter of the room. Feel the change in the entire room once the item has been removed.

Continue to play and experiment with this process until you feel convinced that, indeed, things do have energy and that energy can be felt.

6. Try one more thing (if you dare!): Remove everything from the room. Strip it bare. Furniture, rugs and curtains are all taken out. Request that you be connected with the deva of the room. (Just say aloud: "I'd like to be connected with the deva of this room.") Immediately you may feel an energy shift. This is the deva connecting with you. (If you feel nothing, you're fine. The deva has connected with you per your request, but you are someone who registers energy changes in ways other than by feeling.)

233

Tell the deva the definition, direction and purpose of your room —that is, what it is to be used for and who will be using it. Now request that nature assist you in setting up the room. If you don't already use kinesiology, just follow your intuition. Deal with each item, one at a time, and feel where it's to go and eliminate the items that no longer belong. When you are finished, note the differences in the room arrangement and feel the differences in the room's atmosphere. When the room feels right to you, thank the deva for its help and request that it now disconnect from you. ("Thank you. I'd like to be disconnected from the deva of this room.")

Note the differences between your working on your own to figure out the best arrangement for the room and your working with nature. Now you're starting to experience what it's like to work in a co-creative partnership.

CARING CUSTODIANSHIP OF
THE THINGS AROUND US

So you get an apartment or a room or a house or a hut, and you take all this stuff I'm saying about energy to heart and carefully set out with nature to create a balanced environment for yourself. You and nature "consider" colors, textures, style, arrangement of furniture, trinkets, a few plants and maybe a rock or two. And you end up with a space that makes you feel happy just to walk into. It makes you feel good. You've created a balanced whole—one that is life-supporting and harmonious to all things contained within it, including yourself. In gardening terms, you've done a good job with the interplanting. It's also called manifestation: the careful drawing to oneself exactly what one needs for a harmonious lifestyle.

Then one day your consciousness changes—as consciousness is wont to do. You walk into your home and it doesn't feel as good to you. That's energy. When your consciousness changes, your own energy field makes a corresponding shift. You can't have one without the other. Now, when you walk into your home, things that used to feel harmonious with your energy field are, because of the shift, no longer harmonious. The two fields don't mesh smoothly, and the friction between them makes you feel uncomfortable, tense, tired, irritable or like you don't want to go home. In other words, when you changed your consciousness, you automatically changed the i/e balance in your home. You changed the definition, direction and purpose, and nature immediately adjusted the involution dynamic to match. However, the physical house environment still reflects the old i/e balance. In order to restore balance, you must work with nature to change the house environment to match the new i/e dynamic.

The new friction also registers with the particular things around you. Before, when the home space was balanced, it was in balance for every item in that space. Now some of the items that helped create the old environment are no longer appropriate for the new environment.

If you allow the situation to stay this way for any length of time, the individual energy patterns weaken and begin to deteriorate. They are no longer in a balanced, self-sustaining environment. Plants will die, or fall and shatter all over the place. Bookcases will collapse. Chairs will break. A glass bowl that's been dropped a hundred times will suddenly shatter when you accidentally tap it with a cup.

The best thing to do, before your home comes crashing down around your ears, is to recognize what's happening and make the necessary changes. One important change is to release the things that no longer feel appropriate so that new things that are in harmony with your change in consciousness can come to you. It's clearing out the old to make way for the new. We often feel this in terms of our wardrobe when we feel an intense desire to change styles or not to wear a certain color again.

If you release the old, your ability to draw to yourself and acquire the appropriate new items will be effortless. Manifestation. If you don't release, and you squirrel these things away, your environment becomes stagnant and clogged, and it is very difficult to draw new things to you. In addition, you are acting irresponsibly toward the things you've squirreled away. It's hard for something to fulfill its purpose once it has been stuffed in a box and shoved into a dark corner of the basement.

Appropriate Release

Appropriate release is as tricky as appropriate custodianship. The important thing is to make a clear decision to release and then act on that decision with a sense of clarity and care.

Let's say it is absolutely appropriate to throw something away or recycle it: It is no longer usable in its present form. Once that decision is made, the form's energy shifts—with the aid of the nature spirit level—and the form then continues its life cycle by composting or being changed through recycling to new form with a completely different energy pattern. Nothing dies. It just changes.

Then there are those things that shouldn't be tossed and need to be sold or given away. Once we've made this decision here at Perelandra, we connect with nature and ask that the perfect person in relationship to the item be drawn to us. Usually this occurs immediately, but if it doesn't, we've noticed it's because we have not released the item emotionally. We've still maintained a tie with it and we've clogged up the release process. Once we are emotionally clear, the appropriate person comes along.

In both cases, it is important to release an object in the spirit of gratitude and acknowledgment for the purpose the object has served in our life. With this, we can function as partners with the object, knowing that we are responding to its life cycle. When we follow the process this way, we can actually feel the correctness surrounding the release, and it becomes an exhilarating experience—one of celebration.

Regarding the importance of clarity, I've found that when working with nature it's been absolutely imperative that movement and decisions be made with clarity. This has to do with our role in i/e balance. We provide definition, direction and purpose. If we are hesitant, fearful or indecisive, we create a lack of clarity around the evolution dynamics, thereby making it impossible for nature to provide the best matter, means and action. They can only respond to what we provide. In other words, what we put in is what we get back out.

For example, note the difference in the following: One person asks nature, "Since this tree was so severely damaged by lightning, is it best to cut it down?" Another person says, "I guess I should cut this tree down, but I've always loved it and it's always produced such nice pears and maybe it'll produce a few more next summer—besides, the squirrels have always liked the tree, and if I cut it down where will they go?—and maybe the tree will grow new branches. . . ."

If the tree is not to be cut down, it will be easier for nature to get that message through to the first person because he has asked a simple, direct question and not created "thought pollution." His intentions are clear. And he has given nature a clear opportunity to add its input by asking the question. The second person is so afraid he's going to do something wrong, he's tripping all over himself. He's not asking a question, he's not making a decision, he has no idea what to do. Neither does anyone else—including nature. There's no way information from nature can get in to him.

For myself, I had to learn that it was okay to make a mistake—a good, clear, healthy, down-home mistake. Nature would rather have me attempt to act in partnership and make a mistake as a result, than have me move in confusion, or independently or not act at all. Some of my best insights have come to me out of a mistake—quantum leaps in understanding spring from my disasters!

One more insight regarding "Appropriate Release"—once, after giving the Object Meditation, I asked everyone to share their experiences. One woman's face was pale with fright, so I asked her to show us the object she had used and to explain what had happened. She showed us a ceramic cup—the kind of cup in Japanese tea sets. She said that when she connected with its consciousness, she was immediately blasted with anger, and for the entire time she was connected, she was being chastised. The conversation went something like: "How dare you! How dare you assume the right to enter my consciousness. You have no right. You humans abuse me, misuse me and then you expect me to give you my light and love," etc., etc.

Well, it seemed like a fairly harmless cup to me. But obviously something was wrong. So I asked her for more information. She explained that she had found the cup that day in a sand pile used for mixing cement by a construction site. She liked the cup, so she cleaned it and brought it to the meditation. I suggested that for her to understand the cup's communication, she would have to somehow find out its history: who owned it before, how it was used, how it got to the sand pile, etc.

That's when another person in the group gingerly raised her hand and said that she could give the background. It seems that the cup was part of a Japanese tea set that had been given to her and her husband twelve years earlier as a wedding present. Neither one of them liked the tea set, but they didn't want to give it away for fear of hurting the feelings of the person who had given it to them. So they proceeded to "accidentally" try to break the set. Over the twelve years, they had succeeded in breaking everything but two cups. One was at the construction site holding paint brushes in turpentine. The other was the one found in the sand pile. This was a clear case of irresponsible custodianship and release.

Both cups were given to the woman who liked them. In a short period of time, the anger in the cups' energy pattern was transformed simply by the care and appreciation from their new custodian.

One last point regarding this cup: It certainly sounded from what the woman was reporting that the cup was "hopping mad" and ready to "slap her silly" for using it during the Object Meditation. Although inanimate objects have intelligent consciousness, this does not mean that they become animated cartoons that run around threatening us. During the meditation, per the woman's request, the cup connected her with its full pattern. Those elements of the pattern created by the attitudes and actions of the original owners were the easiest for the woman to recognize, and she translated what she had experienced according to what she understood. Cups simply don't and can't stomp feet at us—they have no feet. But they can reflect to us their full reality in order to show us the impact we humans have on inanimate objects. This woman's experience was a clear and powerful lesson for everyone present at this Object Meditation.

THOUGHT AND COMMUNICATION

Thought is form—a physical vehicle. Silent words. Behind the silent words are patterns of energy without which the words, even though silent, can't exist. In short, thought has order, organization and life vitality.

We initiate communication on an energy level. We draw together the appropriate patterns. Then to make these patterns use-

240

ful, we translate them into form: thought. When we communicate with another person, we convey energy patterns from ourselves to the other person using another vehicle of form: spoken words. The quality of our communication depends on our ability to translate energy patterns into the appropriate words and on the ability of the person receiving the communication to coordinate the words with the energy patterns accompanying it. The sender and the receiver have to translate well. But what's being translated is energy—energy into five-senses form and five-senses form back into energy.

If we did not have a sensory system, we wouldn't need to go through this process. I've experienced, both as a sender and as a receiver, what it is to move communication energy around without attaching five-senses form to it. When I was asked to help the Eastern Orthodox priest just prior to the train accident (Part 2), I didn't sit on top of his consciousness telling him about my experience, word after word after word. All I did was touch into the energy pattern of my experience by recreating it in my memory (which only took a second or two), identify that pattern in its entirety and move the energy as a package into the vibrational field of the priest. What he received was the whole experience in a split second of timing. As he identified the pattern that came into his field, he translated it into his own words.

In everyday communication we still deal with energy, only we add the challenge of transporting it through the use of five-senses form. We've all physically felt that energy from time to time. Someone says something particularly mean or cruel to us, and we feel as if we've been kicked in the stomach by a mule. The words alone certainly didn't do that. We're feeling the effect of their energy that has been charged by the intent of the sender.

241

The Ecological Effects of Thought

As mentioned above, we're quite familiar with what it feels like to be "hit" with someone's thought energy, but we also need to include what happens to the environment when it's hit with thought energy—or any energy coming from us.

I once had a friend who couldn't walk into a specific room in a mutual friend's house without being overwhelmed with a sense of frustration and despair. The room had been recently painted. All the while the husband painted the walls, he had been thinking and worrying about the deep financial difficulties he was experiencing. The energy he released around those thoughts became part of the pattern of the paint and actually crystallized in that pattern as it dried. Frustration and despair were now part of the room's environment.

Another example: A woman walked into an empty room at Findhorn, felt a sudden sense of grief and began to cry—literally to sob. The man who had been in the room before had received word that his father had died of a massive heart attack. The night before he left Findhorn, he stayed up grieving his loss. The energy of grief simply stayed in the room, and this is what the woman had encountered.

During one of the Object Meditations, a young man was connecting with a sweater that his grandmother had knit for him. It was his favorite sweater. As he touched into its energy, he began to experience a heavy, black sensation. He pulled out of the meditation and asked for help. I asked him to give me the history of the sweater. He told me that knitting the sweater was the very last thing his grandmother did before dying. When I asked how she died, he told me that she slowly starved to death. She knit the sweater while she went through this slow, painful death. The vibrations from the experience became an integral part of the energy pattern of the sweater, and it was this that he had connected with during the meditation.

You see, our thoughts don't just affect other people. They affect all things around us. When we deal with energy, we deal with a different dynamic. A word in itself won't affect a lamp. But the energy pattern behind the word can affect the energy pattern behind the lamp. That's the dynamic of energy. It's the same as when my stressful thought forms altered the overall energy pattern of the garden, making it weak and causing the Brussels sprouts to be vulnerable to an infestation of insects.

I'm not suggesting that we all only think rosy thoughts and feel happy emotions. That would be crazy. I've visited places where this is espoused, but it only succeeds in making everyone tense and emotionally constipated. I feel it's an unnatural thing to ask of anyone. Life includes a full spectrum of experiences and emotions. Aside from this, we're all in a state of transition. We're growing and changing in awareness on all levels, including emotional. Much to some people's surprise, we're not perfect. We don't always know how to express ourselves in balance. But we are learning—slowly. And that's okay. In the meantime, we need to recognize the fact that we are capable of affecting the environment adversely as we go through our growth and changes, and we need to develop techniques for cleaning up and taking care of our pollution.

Keep in mind what we're working with—energy that has been released into our environment by us. As a result, these energies have become a part of that environment. Say, for example, I grieve. It is a natural reaction to death. From me flows the energy of grief. If I don't know how to include a feeling of love, joy and appreciation for that person as part of my grief, I then experience the process as just deep pain. I have excluded those elements of the process that include love, joy and appreciation. If I walk out of a room having only felt pain, I leave behind the energy of that pain as part of the room's environment. That energy then maintains the character of the pain of that moment and becomes part of the environment of the room.

The problem we face is how to release that energy without manipulating it. In the above examples, I pointed out frustration and despair that had become part of wall paint, grief that was "left behind" in a room and despair that led to starvation that became part of a sweater. There is no need to deal with the situations by torching the rooms or the sweater. We humans introduced the emotional energy into the patterns of these forms and we humans can release them.

Some people attempt to release emotional energy from a room by burning candles or incense—or both. But I find this ineffectual. It's a hit-and-miss process designed to place distance between us and the energy we wish to move. There is a prejudice that sometimes develops toward these energies: They're dirty. They're dangerous. They're something we "high-souled" humans shouldn't get near. We tend to forget that we created them. And just because grief, for example, left as only an energy of deep pain has an effect on its surrounding environment, doesn't mean that grief is dirty or dangerous.

In my own search for answers to this situation, nature worked with me to develop the Energy Cleansing Process for the removal of inappropriate energies causing imbalance in all form. It may sound odd that nature is involved in this, but the energy we create and leave behind affects all that falls under nature's domain—including these energies themselves. All of nature, all objects, all form on Earth are included in the "nature department." If we're to work responsibly and with a sense of cooperation in any process involved in this area, it must be with the aid of nature.

In this process, we remove energy by using energy. Don't get nervous—it's quite simple. One of the easiest ways to move energy around is through visualization. If you want to move energy from point A to point B, visualize the energy at point A, then see it moving to point B. By visualizing energy at point A, then seeing it move to point B, you define what you are working with (energy and two points), give direction by visualizing where it is to move from and to, and add purpose by including your need to work with this energy for a particular situation, experiment or exercise. Nature automatically responds to your evolution input and provides the shift. *It is that simple.*

The only limitation you have in visualization is your own lack of willingness to be creative. It is easier to maintain focus if we make the visualization interesting, even humorous. For example, you can visualize a little train sitting on point A. Visualize a little man shoveling energy into the train, then see the train move to point B. The same little man (who rode on the train to point B) can now unload the energy. The trick is to make the visualization interesting enough so that your focus can be effortlessly maintained. However, you defeat the purpose if you create an elaborate visualization with so much detail that it overwhelms your ability to maintain focus. In essence, you'll experience visualization overload. If this should occur, simplify the visualization.

In order to visualize anything we must draw together the energy to support the visualization. This is not some imaginary, flaky trick I'm talking about. It is i/e balance at work. Because of the dynamics of energy, we can move it around by using visualization as the tool. Just remember that for everything we visualize, nature draws together the corresponding energy—or we won't be able to visualize it. So, in the second example, not only was the original energy moved from point A to point B, but the extra energy of the train, the little man and his shovel, were also moved.

ENERGY MOVEMENT EXERCISE

The following Energy Movement Exercise is designed to give you the experience of moving energy and to help you sharpen your focusing tool.

1. Sit quietly. Close your eyes.

2. See point A on the left of your inner field of vision. If you don't see it, simply place a dot or see a spot and declare that to be point A.

3. Shift your focus to the right side of your field of vision and see point B.

4. At point A, see a ball of energy. See it round, white and the size of a golf ball.

5. Roll the ball of energy to point B. Roll it slowly and keep your focus on it while it moves toward point B.

6. Roll it back to point A. Always keep your focus on the ball while it's in transit. (Roll the ball back and forth until you feel comfortable with the action and can follow it with ease as it rolls, without losing it or letting your focus drift from it. If you lose the ball, simply focus on what you're doing, see the ball again and allow it to continue rolling.)

If you wish to go on:
7. See the ball at point A. Slowly roll the ball from point A to your own left hand. Just visualize the ball moving (with your eyes closed) and see it touch your hand. (Don't be surprised if you actually feel the ball of energy touch your hand.)

8. Once the ball has reached your left hand, slowly move it up your left arm to your shoulder, across the chest to the right shoulder, then down the right arm to the right hand. (Remember: Move the ball slowly. If you lose it, or if your visualization drifts, simply bring your focus back to where you last saw it, see the ball again and move it on. Again, don't be surprised if you feel energy move across your body.)

9. See the ball in the right hand. Move it from that hand back to point B.

10. Release the energies by stating that the visualization is over, and shift your focus by looking at the room around you.

If you find after trying this exercise several times that you simply can't "see" anything, then try it again and just sense the movement of energy. Some people work better by feeling energy rather than by seeing it. In both cases, the quality and clarity of moving energy from point A to point B are directly related to the quality of your focus. In other words, the quality of the evolution input you provide is directly related to the quality of the involution dynamic you get back from nature. If you are sloppy or unsure, or you have a half-hearted, fuzzed-out focus, the energy just isn't going to get to point B. Or only a portion of the energy will make it. The clearer you are and the sharper your focus, the more nature can respond—and the energy will move accordingly.

This little exercise is actually a lot of work. It requires quiet and concentration. It calls into action the various tools we need to begin working with energy: concentration, focus, clarity of visualization and clarity of movement. At the same time, we are developing tools we need for working in partnership with nature: concentration, clarity and focus.

It also emphasizes the relationship between the quality of focus we maintain in the exercise and the quality of relaxation we are in during the exercise. Focus is an action. Quality of focus is enhanced when there are no disturbances to interfere with it. Things perceived by our five senses, such as sound and motion, can disturb focus. So, too, can we be disturbed by our own body when it's not relaxed. When our muscles are in a state of tension, they radiate an energy similar to static electricity, and it's this energy that affects our ability to focus. As you practice the Energy Movement Exercise and as you learn more about what it means for you to get into a comfortable, relaxed position, you will find that it will be easier to hold your focus, and you won't lose the ball of energy nearly as often.

To aid you in your understanding of what is involved in achieving body relaxation, I include another experiential exercise.

RELAXATION EXERCISE

Lie down on the floor on your back. Use a mat or lie on a rug for comfort. Give yourself permission to relax.

Bring your focus in on your breathing . . . feel it as you inhale and exhale. Feel it slowly and steadily as it fills the chest. . . . Focus on the toes of your left foot. Feel each toe separately. . . . Allow the tension to slip away from each toe. . . . Focus on your left foot. Relax each muscle on the top of the foot . . . the sides . . . and the bottom of the foot. Allow the tension to slip right out of the toes. . . . Bring your focus to your left ankle. Unlock the joint and relax it. . . . Relax the calf . . . the front of the calf . . . the sides . . . the back of the calf. . . . Feel your left knee. Unlock the joint and relax it. . . . Move your focus to your left thigh. Relax the muscles in the front . . . on the sides . . . and in the back of the thigh. . . . Now feel the whole left leg heavy and fully supported by the floor.

Focus on your right foot. . . . Feel each toe separately and allow the tension to release from each one. . . . Allow the muscles in the right foot to relax . . . the top of the foot . . . the sides . . . and the bottom of the foot. Bring your focus to your right ankle. . . . Unlock the joint and allow it to relax. . . . Focus on the calf. . . . Relax the front . . . the sides . . . and the back. Move your focus to your right knee. Unlock the joint and relax it. . . . Allow it to be supported by the floor. . . . Relax your right thigh . . . the front . . . the sides . . . and the back of the thigh. . . . Feel the entire right leg heavy and fully supported by the floor. . . . Both the right and left legs should feel heavy.

Bring your focus to your torso. Allow your buttocks to spread into the floor. . . . Relax the pelvic area . . . and your abdomen. Feel the muscles soften. . . . Allow your lower back to relax right into the floor. Release the arch and allow the lower back to sink into the floor. . . . Relax the middle back . . . the upper back . . . and the shoulder blades. Feel the entire back open softly and allow it to be fully supported by the floor. . . . Focus on the chest . . . soften the muscles and allow the rib cage to soften and drop toward the floor. . . . Relax the shoulders and upper chest. . . . Allow the shoulders to drop. Feel the space between the ears and shoulders. . . .

Focus on the fingers of your left hand. Feel each finger and allow the tension to simply slip out of the tip. . . . Focus on the top of the hand and relax it . . . the palm of the left hand. . . . Relax it. . . . Unlock the wrist. . . . Relax the lower arm. . . . Unlock the elbow. . . . Relax the upper arm. . . . Feel the left shoulder relax again. . . . Focus on the right hand. . . . Release the tension from each finger . . . from the top of the hand . . . and from the palm of the hand. . . . Unlock the right wrist. . . . Release the lower arm. . . . Unlock the elbow. . . . Relax the upper arm. . . . Feel the right shoulder relax again.

Focus on the neck. . . . Release the muscles in front . . . the muscles on each side . . . and the muscles in back. . . . Feel the neck supported by the floor. As the neck relaxes, allow that sensation to flow from the neck into the chest, the shoulders and the upper back. . . .

Bring your focus to your head. . . . Sense the head . . . the entire head. Include the ears. Allow the tensions of the day to gently release. . . . Focus on the back of the head . . . feel it soften. . . . Relax the top of the head . . . the forehead. . . . Now the face . . . the jaw . . . mouth . . . tongue . . . eyebrows . . . and the eyes. Feel the eyes relax and feel the sensation of them sinking heavily to the back of the head. See the darkness. . . .

251

Focus on your breathing once again. . . . Inhale . . . Exhale . . . Feel the breath travel through the body as you inhale. Allow the breath to exit your feet as you exhale. . . . Continue to inhale and exhale in a slow, steady rhythm. . . . While you are this relaxed, allow yourself to record the sensation. Note the difference from when you first lay down.

Before moving to get up, sense the room around you. Feel the four walls—feel the floor beneath you. Sense its hardness and actually feel it contact your body. Slowly move your fingers and toes, then your hands and feet. Open your eyes and look around you. When you're ready, slowly sit up, then stand. . . . Walk around a bit and feel the differences in your movement before going about the rest of your day.

When starting out with the Relaxation Exercise and the Energy Movement Exercise, remember that you are working, that you are developing new disciplines, and it would help to be patient with yourself. Your ability to do both exercises improves with practice. Also, if you have a friend handy, it helps to have him or her slowly read off the steps of the exercise as you go through it. That way you don't have to be concerned with trying to remember what comes next—that creates tension. If a friend isn't handy, record the steps of the exercise on a tape recorder for yourself.

SIMPLIFIED ENERGY CLEANSING PROCESS:
Preparation

I refer to this process as the "Simplified Energy Cleansing Process" because it does not include some of the steps—namely, the coning setup and the balancing and stabilizing steps that were included in the full Energy Cleansing Process in the *Perelandra Garden Workbook*. Both versions work extremely well. The simplified version is an excellent way to get started with your co-creative partnership with nature and to experience the effects of that partnership on your environment. And this is what *Behaving* is all about—getting started. (If you wish to use the full Energy Cleansing Process and experience working with nature in deeper and more complete ways, work with the steps as they are written in the *Perelandra Garden Workbook*.)

For the simplified process, you will need to choose the area you want to cleanse. It can be any size, but I suggest you start small until after you have had several experiences with the process and you feel comfortable with the concept. I've cleansed anything from a single, small object to an entire community that was spread out in five different locations, one of which was not even in the same country.

It is important that you be able to close your eyes and easily visualize whatever it is that you are cleansing. If it's a room, you'll need to visualize the shape and layout of the room. If it's a house, you must have a clear sense of the layout of the rooms and the shape of the house. For land, a farm or a community, the distance and shape of the outside boundary is important—plus the relative position of any buildings on the land. For anything larger than one room, I would suggest strongly that you sketch a layout of what you're working with. Nothing elaborate is needed

—for land, a simple line sketch of the shape of the property with the relative placement of the buildings on the property will do. For a home in the suburbs on a small piece of land, a sketch of the shape of the property plus a rectangle where the house is and maybe an indication of where the doghouse, the flower beds and the driveway are. Anything you feel will give you a simple but accurate idea of what you're working with.

The Importance of Attitude: Recognize that it's a very special moment when we become active participants in the rebalancing of our environment. It should not be done haphazardly or hurriedly. The biggest mistake we can make is to slip into manipulation. If we forget that we are aiming to act responsibly in this thing we call life and that we are choosing to participate as equal partners with nature with the life around us, we can very easily slip from a spirit of co-creation to one of manipulation. Then we would not be participating in a process of balance and gentleness but one of force and domination. Consequently, the attitude we have as we enter this is vitally important and a key to maintaining a sense of balance while going through the cleansing process.

Another point: It is not appropriate to do the Energy Cleansing Process (simplified or complete) on land that you do not own or are not renting. In an office building, it is only appropriate to do the program for your office or work space, not the entire building. It is never appropriate to decide for others what is best for them, even if you think the Energy Cleansing Process is the most beneficial thing around. Focus only on the environments for which you are directly responsible and don't impose this process on others without their conscious permission.

Simplified Energy Cleansing Process

1. Choose and diagram the area to be cleansed. Place the diagram in front of you during the process. (If you need to clarify your visualization of what you're cleansing, you'll be able to look at the diagram and refresh your memory.)

2. Sit or lie quietly. Focus on relaxing your body. Either do the full Relaxation Exercise or an abbreviation of it. When complete, focus as you inhale and exhale a few times. Then state to yourself or aloud, "I would like to do a Simplified Energy Cleansing Process."

3. With your eyes closed, see a bright, white beam of light above your head. This is the light of the christ.* See the light rays from that beam move down toward you and totally envelop you in white light.
   State to yourself or aloud,
   "I ask that the light of the christ (evolutionary light) aid me so that what I am about to do will be for the highest good. I ask that this light help me in transmuting any inappropriate and ungrounded energies released by us humans and that I be protected fully during this process. I welcome your presence and thank you for your help."

4. Focus again above your head. See a second beam of light, a green light. This is the light of nature or the involution dynamic

---

* If you have difficulty using this phrase for the white light, refer to it as "the evolutionary light." "Light of the christ" is ancient terminology that has only recently come into question. It was originally used to describe the evolutionary dynamic contained within us all, and originally did not refer to the religious figure, Jesus Christ.

contained within all form). See the green light totally envelop you, commingling with the white light. (The quality of the light simply depends on the quality of your focus. If the light isn't very bright, see it brighter. Or *will* yourself to see it brighter.)

State (to yourself or aloud),

"I ask that the light of nature aid me in releasing and collecting the energies absorbed by the nature kingdoms, tangible and intangible, animate and inanimate. I also ask that the light of nature aid me so that what I am about to do will be for the highest good. I welcome your presence and thank you for your help."

5. State,

"I ask that any inappropriate, stagnant, darkened or ungrounded energies be released from this area. I request that the process proceed *gently*, knowing that the cleansing and transmutation process I am about to be a part of is a process of life, of evolution and not negation."

6. Now, shift your focus and visualize the area to be cleansed. (If you're having trouble, sneak a peek at your diagram.) Visualize the shape of the area, especially the outside boundaries.

7. Next, visualize a thin white sheet of light forming five feet *below* the lowest point of your area. (If it's a house or a piece of land, see the sheet form five feet underground. If you are not sure where the lowest point is, simply request that this sheet form five feet below the area's lowest point, wherever that is.) See the sheet brighten and become whiter. Focus on it until it is bright and clear. Allow the outside edges of the sheet to extend five feet *beyond* the outside boundary of the area.

8. Once the sheet is fully formed, ask that the light of the christ (evolutionary light) and the light of nature join you as together you *slowly* move the sheet up and through the area to be cleansed. See the sheet move slowly, evenly and *with ease*. (Remember, energy moves easily through form.) Stay focused on the sheet and watch it move through the area. If the sheet moves too slowly, too quickly, or one side is not rising at the same height, ask that the sheet stop, request any specific changes needed and then ask that the sheet continue to be raised. The changes you requested will be in place. As the sheet moves through the area, see the pockets of released energy collecting on it. Don't feel you have to fantasize these energies. They will automatically collect in the sheet. All you have to do is recognize their presence.

Allow the sheet to rise to five feet *above* the highest point of the area you are cleansing—the top of the room, a tree, the roof, the highest hill—and then stop.

9. State, "I now wish to create a bundle with the sheet." Visualize you and nature carefully gathering the edges of the sheet, forming a bundle of white light that totally encloses the collected energies. To the left of the bundle see the gold cord from the light of the christ (evolutionary light). Tie the bundle closed with this cord. To the right of the sheet, see the gold cord from the light of nature, and tie it around the top of the bundle along with the first cord.

10. State,
  "I now release the bundle to the light of the christ (evolutionary light) and the light of nature, so that the energies that have been released can be moved to their next higher level

for transmutation and the continuation of their own evolutionary process."

Watch the bundle lift. *Important:* Just watch. Don't try to determine where the next higher level is.

11. Return your focus to the now-cleansed area. Observe the area and feel, sense or see any changes.

12. Shift your focus to your breathing, focusing on your body as you inhale and exhale slowly three or four times.

13. Spend a moment recognizing all the energies that came together as a result of your intent and focus, and that cooperated with you throughout the process:

> The white light of the christ
> The green light of nature
> The white sheet
> The gold cords
> The energies that were released

In the spirit of gratitude, request that these energies fully release from your focus. (This will occur immediately.) Focus on your breathing once again.

14. Shift your focus to the room around you. Sense the walls. The floor. Feel whatever your body is touching. Wiggle your toes and fingers. Slowly move your hands and feet. Open your eyes and look at the room around you. When you're ready, slowly rise to your feet. Walk around. Look out a window. Give yourself a moment before continuing your day. Be sure you feel absolutely present to yourself. If you feel "spacey," walk outside and put your hands on a tree or a rock, focusing on your sensation of touch with it. Just continue moving your hands over it until you

can clearly feel it. Or spend time smelling a flower. Or drink a glass of water. In essence, simply ground yourself by focusing on your five senses.

When finished, take time to feel the area you have cleansed. Some people sense fresher-smelling air. Sometimes they smell the aroma of flowers. Or they'll feel the room as being "lighter." Also, you may have felt the sheet as it moved through you. Frequently others in the area who aren't even participating in the process will have a sensation of something moving through them. It's not an unpleasant feeling at all, since everything that occurs during the process is in balance. And any inappropriate energies that were in their field will have also been released to the sheet.

The easiest way to get through the Simplified Energy Cleansing Process, especially in the beginning, is by recording the steps on tape, remembering to give yourself plenty of time to complete each step. *In order to maintain the co-creative balance in the process, it's important that no step be altered or eliminated.* It might be helpful to have the tape machine within easy reach so that it can be turned off while the sheet is rising, giving you all the time you need. If more than one person wants to be involved, allow one person to read the steps and guide everyone else through the process together. If this is done, it's important that the reader try to be sensitive to everyone in the room and keep them moving through the process as a group.

However often you do the Simplified Energy Cleansing Process is up to you and your perception of how often an area needs it. However, here are my recommendations that you might find helpful: For a home, I would suggest weekly. If you or someone else in your environment is going through a difficult or emotional time, it may be appropriate to cleanse the area more frequently. A professional therapist, counselor, chiropractor or massage therapist, for example, should consider doing the process on a daily basis. The Simplified Energy Cleansing Process not only assists the balance of the natural environment, but also assists our ability to maintain equilibrium on all levels by surrounding us with a balanced support environment and allowing us the opportunity to move through personal process without constantly bumping into collected emotional energy that may or may not have anything to do with the present situation.

For Additional Help: If you discover that you are having trouble finding someone to read these exercises aloud for you or feel you can't record them on tape to your own satisfaction, you may wish to phone, fax or write to us at Perelandra for a current catalog. I have made tapes of several exercises, including the ones in this book. You'll find Perelandra's address and phone numbers in the Afterword.

AFTERWORD

Since the first publication of *Behaving*, I have made the process of working in a co-creative partnership not only easier but more foolproof, as well. We all have intuition, but relying on it for the kind of precise, in-depth information you'll need from nature for working in a co-creative partnership is difficult. Even knowing the kinds of questions we can ask nature can be tough. The *Perelandra Garden Workbook* and the *Perelandra Garden Workbook II* break down everything I do in my co-creative partnership and present it in easy-to-follow steps. Also, I have included the sessions I had with nature that explain the processes, the concepts behind them and why they work. And I list the various questions to ask. You use kinesiology (muscle testing) as the communication tool for getting nature's input, which allows you to get the kind of in-depth information you need. You can begin your partnership by simply declaring your intent as described in Part 4. But as soon as you get that partnership rolling, I strongly recommend that you use the *Workbook*s for moving it onto the practical, day-to-day level. In short, the framework for co-creative partnerships has already been developed, and you are not required to re-invent that wheel. All you have to do is do it.

PERELANDRA TODAY

Perelandra now consists of forty-five acres of open fields and woods in the foothills of the Blue Ridge Mountains in Virginia, and is both home for Clarence and me, and a private nature research center. Since 1976, I have continued to work with nature intelligences in a coordinated, co-creative and educational effort that has resulted in understanding and demonstrating a new approach to agriculture and ecological balance. Perelandra has developed into a research center in the truest sense of the word. The main focus of the research is centered in the one-hundred-foot-diameter garden. It functions as a laboratory, and it is here that I get from nature the information I need to create an all-inclusive garden environment based on the principles of balance. For example, we do not attempt to repel insects. Instead, we focus on creating a balanced environment—nature defines the makeup, patterns and rhythms of this balanced environment—that attracts and fully supports a complete and appropriate population of insects. In turn, the insects relate to the garden's plant life in a light and nondestructive manner. Each year is different and builds on the foundation laid the previous years.

From this work has developed a new method of gardening that I call "co-creative gardening." Briefly, this is a method of gardening in partnership with nature intelligences that emphasizes balance and teamwork. The balance is a result of concentrating on the laws of nature and form *from nature's perspective*. The teamwork is established between the individual and the intelligent levels inherent in nature. Both of these point out the differences between co-creative agriculture and traditional organic gardening or agricultural methods. And it is from this new method of gardening that come the principles, insights and lessons that can be applied by anyone in any "garden" environment.

In late fall 1984, we expanded the research to include the garden known as the human body, and we began developing and producing the Perelandra Rose Essences. These are a set of eight flower essences that function in coordination with one another to support and balance an individual as he proceeds in day-to-day evolutionary process. The eight essences are co-creatively produced, and they benefit additionally by being produced from roses grown in the Perelandra garden.

Since 1984, we have produced four more sets of Perelandra Essences: the Perelandra Garden Essences, the Perelandra Rose Essences II, the Perelandra Nature Program Essences and the

Perelandra Soul Ray Essences. Also, this expanded research has led to new insight in our understanding of the role nature plays in our personal health and well-being and has resulted in two major health programs: MAP and the Perelandra Microbial Balancing Program.*

My research with nature has led to the development of a new science I call "co-creative science." Traditional science is man's study of reality and how it works. Co-creative science is the study of reality and how it works by man and nature working together in a conscious partnership.

My education has been only a part of what has gone on here. The fact that Perelandra is a research center and the garden its laboratory has given the nature intelligences a place in which to work out natural law in new ways that better address the environmental issues we presently face. Much of our published material is a result of this particular area of focus.

The term "research center" has caused many to think that we are a community and open to the public. We are not. We are a private research center and we have no plans to expand to a traditional community.

We feel it is important to maintain an environment that will facilitate and enhance the research: calm and quiet. The best way to accommodate the research as well as the many requests to visit Perelandra is to have several annual open houses during the summer and early fall. Aside from these open houses, *Perelandra is closed to the public*. We cannot accommodate unannounced or

---

* We have published books detailing both programs. For a current book list, see the Bibliography at the end of this book or contact us for a current catalog for information about the books and the Perelandra Essences.

unscheduled visits. We appreciate your understanding in this and hope that the open houses address your need to visit and experience Perelandra.

We have had to consider how to maintain the proper research environment while we get information to others so that they may begin implementing it in their lives. It is a tricky balance. This is where our catalog and web site come in. There is much going on here and we feel our most efficient and effective means for sharing the Perelandra information is through the catalog and the web site. If you would like our catalog (there is no charge for the catalog), here's how to contact us:

24-Hour Ordering Phone Numbers:
U.S. and Canada: 1-800-960-8806
Overseas and Mexico: 1-540-937-2153
24-Hour Fax Line: 1-540-937-3360
Our address: P.O. Box 3603, Warrenton, VA 20188
And if you are a net surfer, you can get our entire current
catalog plus other information: http://www.perelandra-ltd.com

We have a terrific staff who will respond to your request right away. We look forward to this vital outreach with you and hope there is something we offer that helps you in your personal understanding and relationship with the world of nature.

Machaelle Small Wright
Perelandra
March 1997

BIBLIOGRAPHY

Books by Machaelle Small Wright
All books published by Perelandra, Ltd.

Behaving as if the God in All Life Mattered (revised edition)

Dancing in the Shadows of the Moon

Co-Creative Science: A Revolution in Science Providing Real Solutions for Today's Health and Environment

Perelandra Garden Workbook: A Complete Guide to Gardening with Nature Intelligences (second edition)

Perelandra Garden Workbook II: Co-Creative Energy Processes for Gardening, Agriculture and Life

Flower Essences: Reordering Our Understanding and Approach to Illness and Health

MAP: The Co-Creative White Brotherhood Medical Assistance Program (second edition)

Perelandra Microbial Balancing Program Manual (second edition)

Other publications mentioned in *Behaving* that are still available:

The Findhorn Community. *The Findhorn Garden.*
HarperCollins Publishers
10 East 53rd St.
New York, NY 10022

Lorusso, Julie and Joel Glick. *Healing Stoned: The Therapeutic Use of Gems and Minerals*
Brotherhood of Life Books, 2nd Edition (1995)
P.O. Box 46306
Las Vegas, NV 89114-6306

Maclean, Dorothy. *To Hear the Angels Sing: An Odyssey of Co-Creation with the Devic Kingdom.*
Lindisfarne Press (1990)
R.R. 4, Box 94A1
Hudson, NY 12534